T0009228

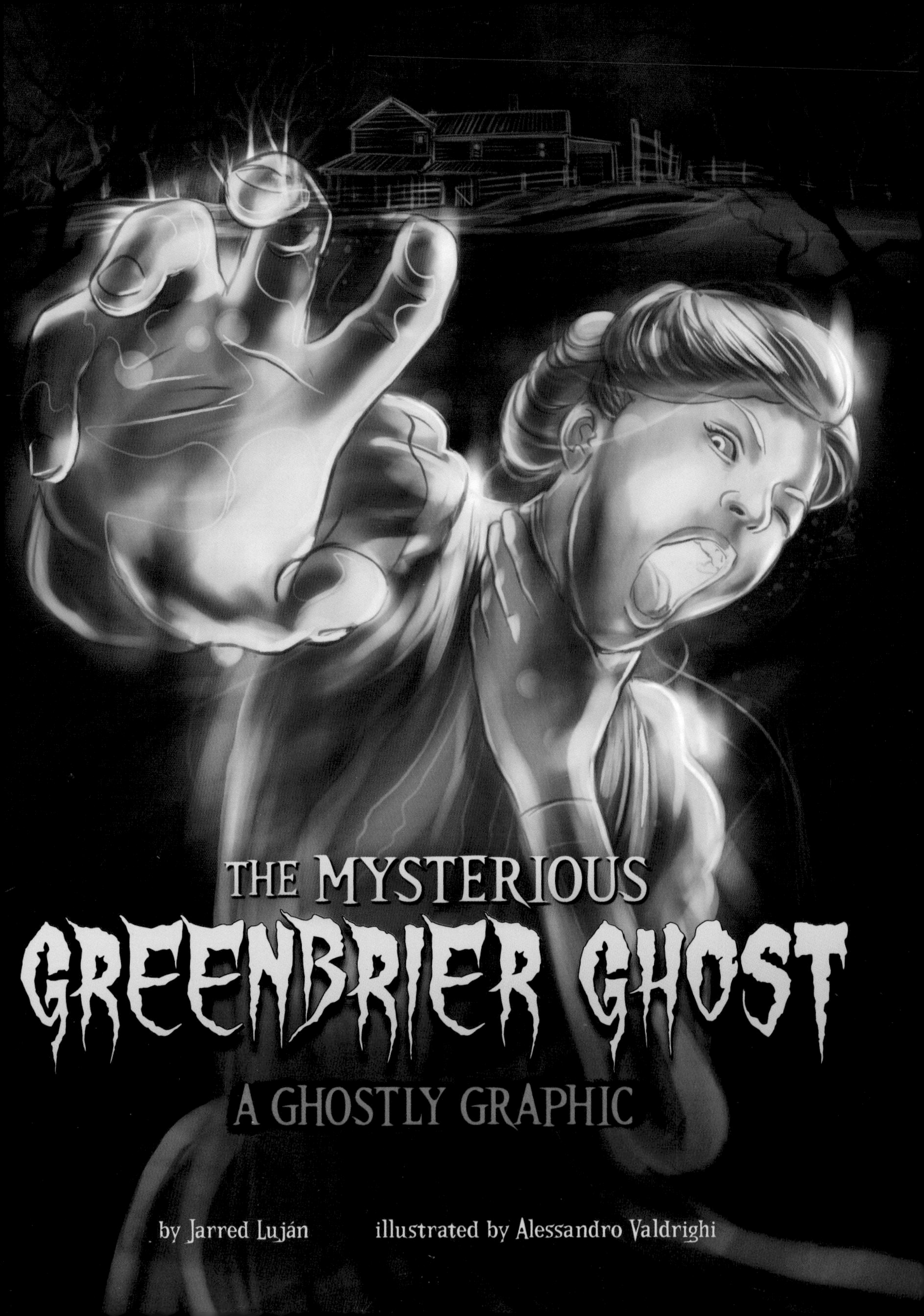

# THE MYSTERIOUS GREENBRIER GHOST

## A GHOSTLY GRAPHIC

by Jarred Luján illustrated by Alessandro Valdrighi

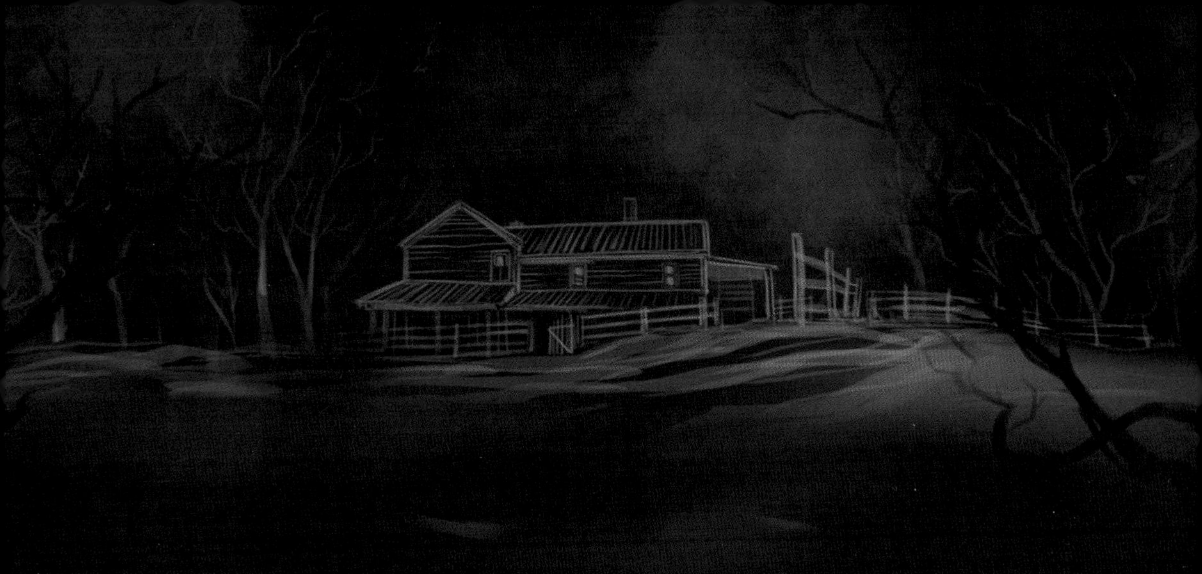

# THE MYSTERIOUS GREENBRIER GHOST

## A GHOSTLY GRAPHIC

by Jarred Luján
illustrated by Alessandro Valdrighi

CAPSTONE PRESS
a capstone imprint

Published by Capstone Press, an imprint of Capstone
1710 Roe Crest Drive, North Mankato, Minnesota 56003
capstonepub.com

Library of Congress Cataloging-in-Publication Data
is available on the Library of Congress website.

ISBN: 9781669068464 (hardcover)
ISBN: 9781669071365 (paperback)
ISBN: 9781669068488 (ebook PDF)

Summary: In 1897, Zona Shue was found dead at the bottom of a
staircase in Greenbrier County, West Virginia. Heart failure was listed as her
cause of death—but Zona's soul could not rest. Soon her ghost visited her
mother to deliver a ghoulish message. She had been murdered! Could the
words of Zona's restless spirit be trusted? And would they lead authorities
to a cold-blooded killer?

Editorial Credits
Editor: Christopher Harbo; Designer: Sarah Bennett;
Production Specialist: Katy LaVigne

Printed and bound in the USA. 5853

# TABLE OF CONTENTS

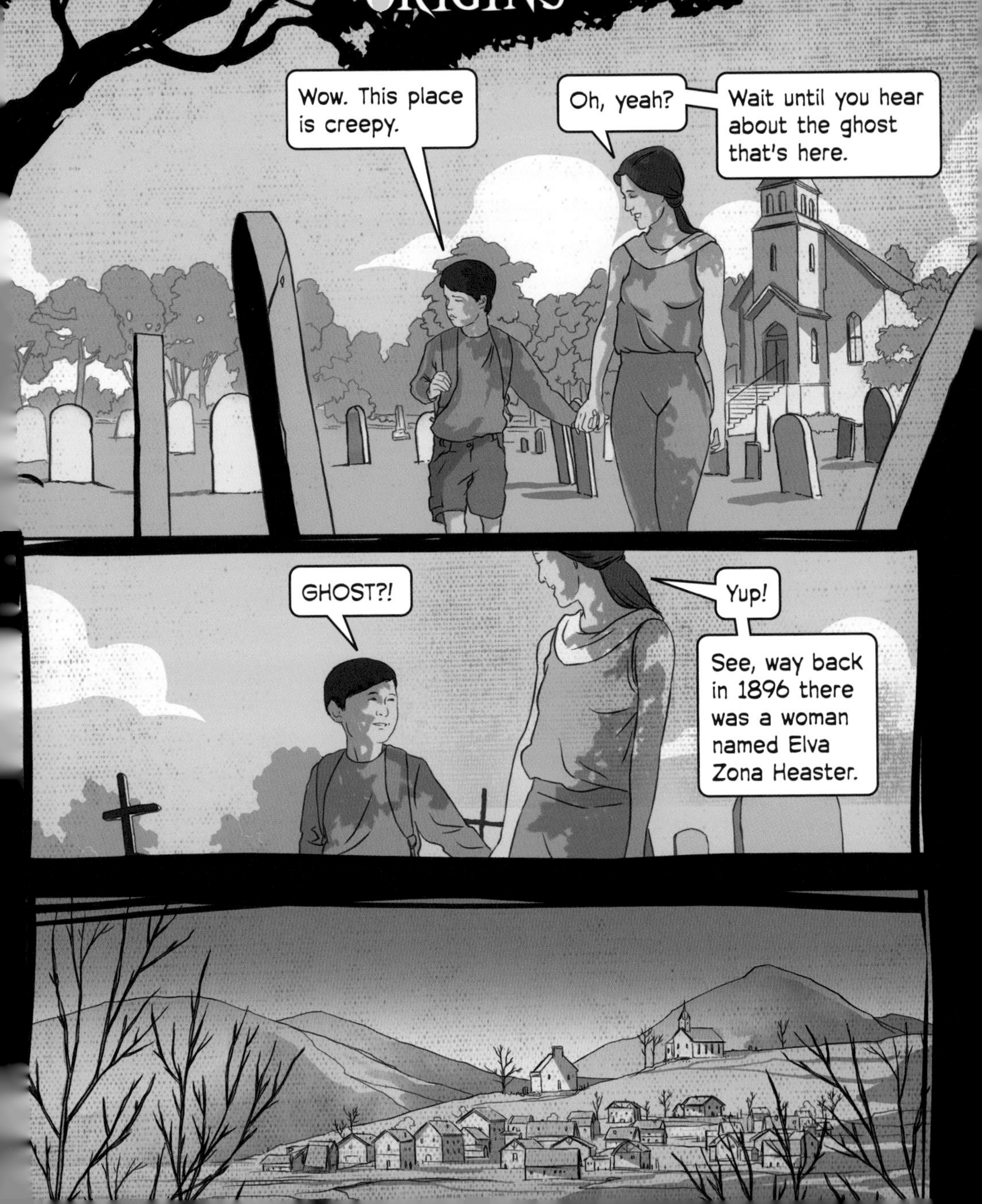
Wow. This place is creepy.
Oh, yeah?
Wait until you hear about the ghost that's here.
GHOST?!
Yup!
See, way back in 1896 there was a woman named Elva Zona Heaster.

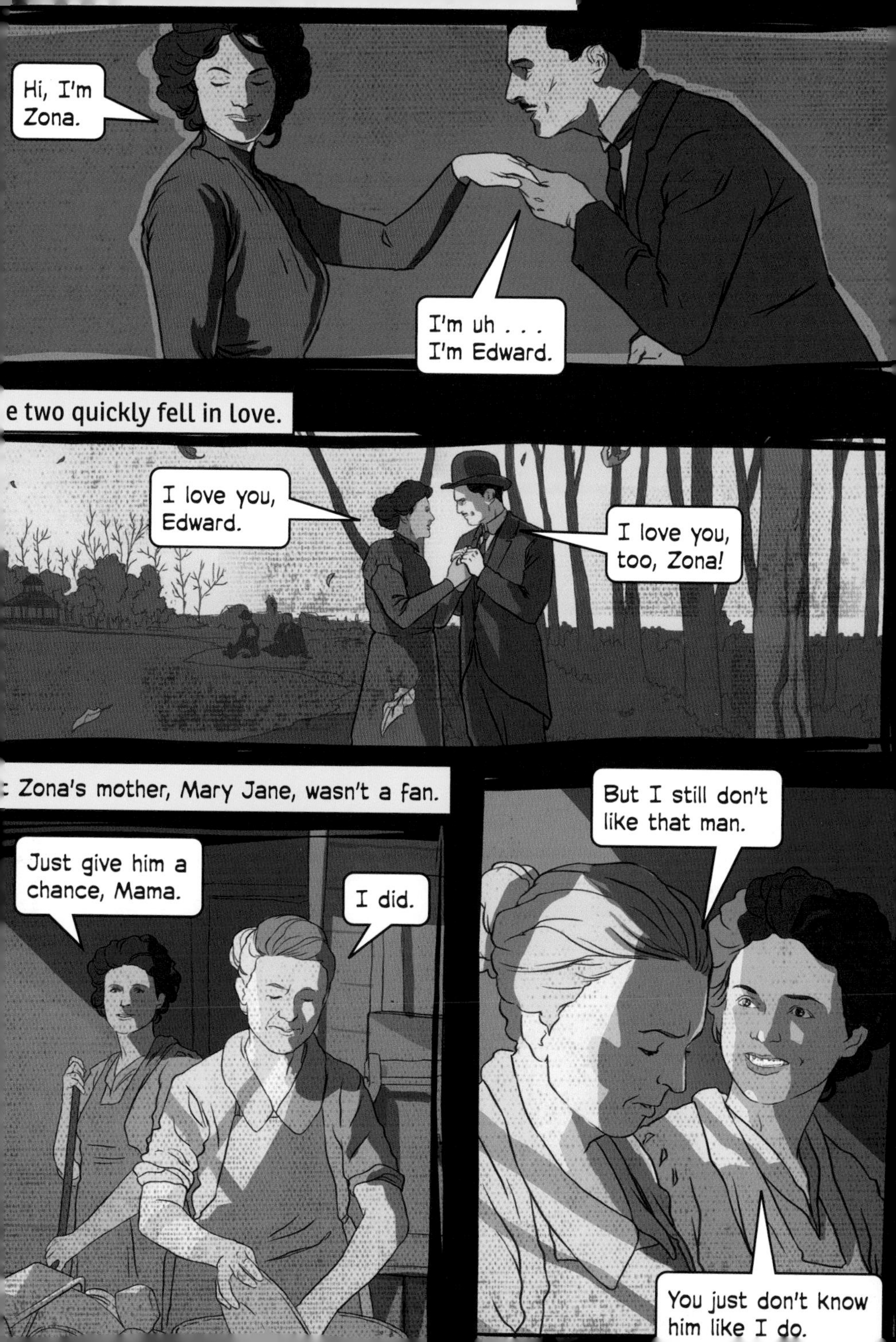
Hi, I'm Zona.
I'm uh . . . I'm Edward.
e two quickly fell in love.
I love you, Edward.
I love you, too, Zona!
Zona's mother, Mary Jane, wasn't a fan.
Just give him a chance, Mama.
I did.
But I still don't like that man.
You just don't know him like I do.

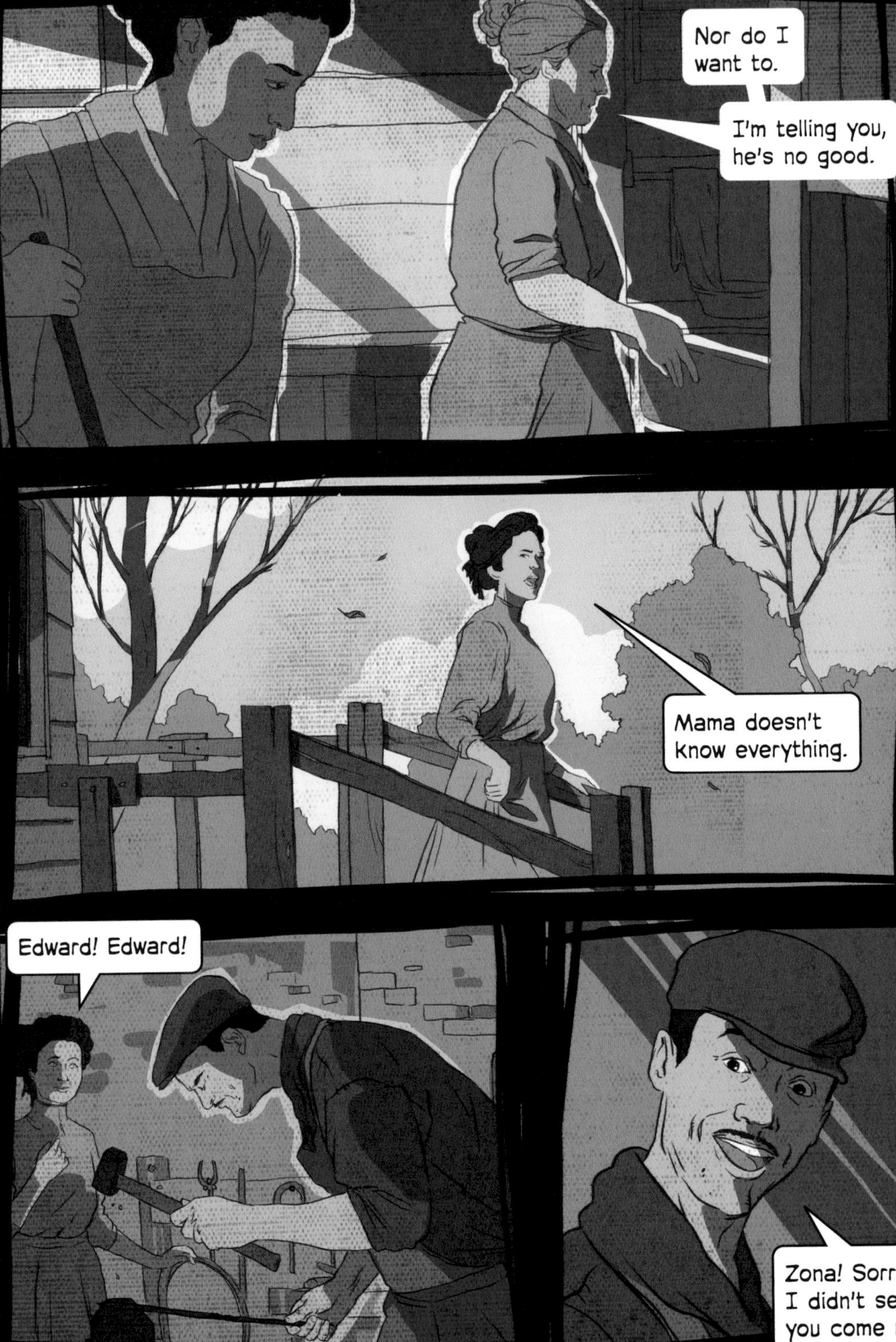
Nor do I want to.
I'm telling you, he's no good.
Mama doesn't know everything.
Edward! Edward!
Zona! Sorr
I didn't se
you come

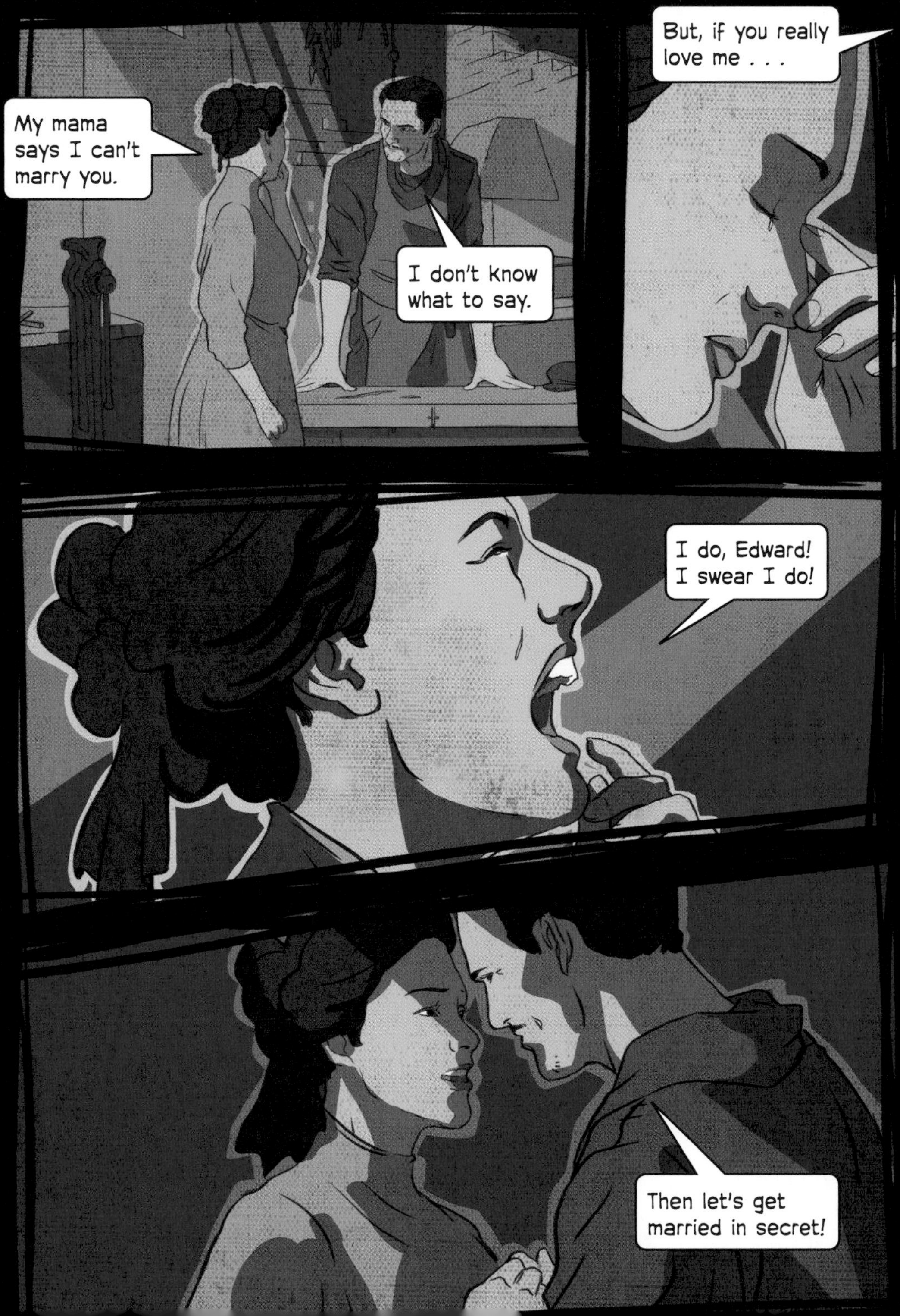
My mama says I can't marry you.
I don't know what to say.
But, if you really love me . . .
I do, Edward! I swear I do!
Then let's get married in secret!

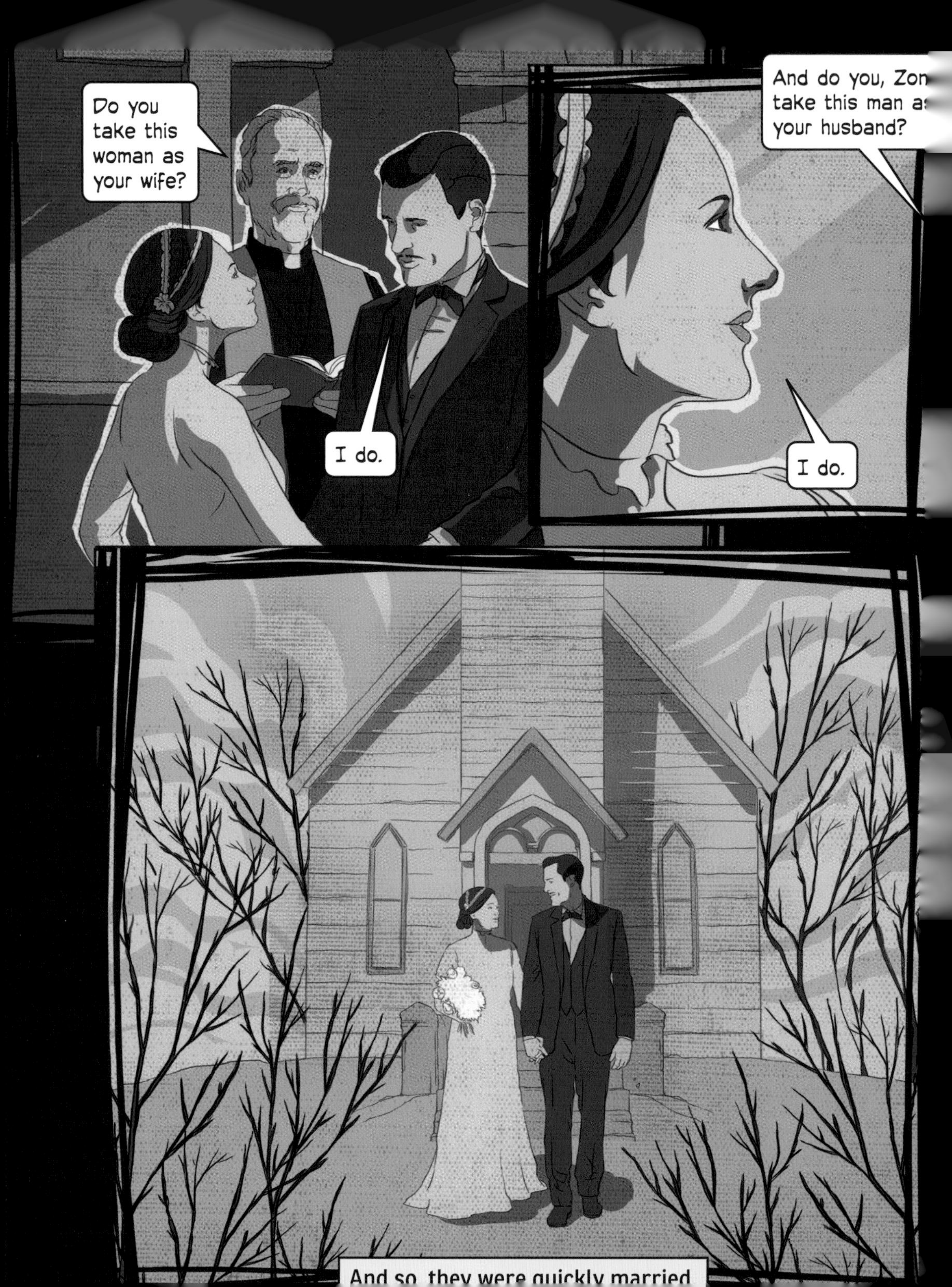
Do you take this woman as your wife?
I do.
And do you, Zon
take this man a
your husband?
I do.
And so, they were quickly married.

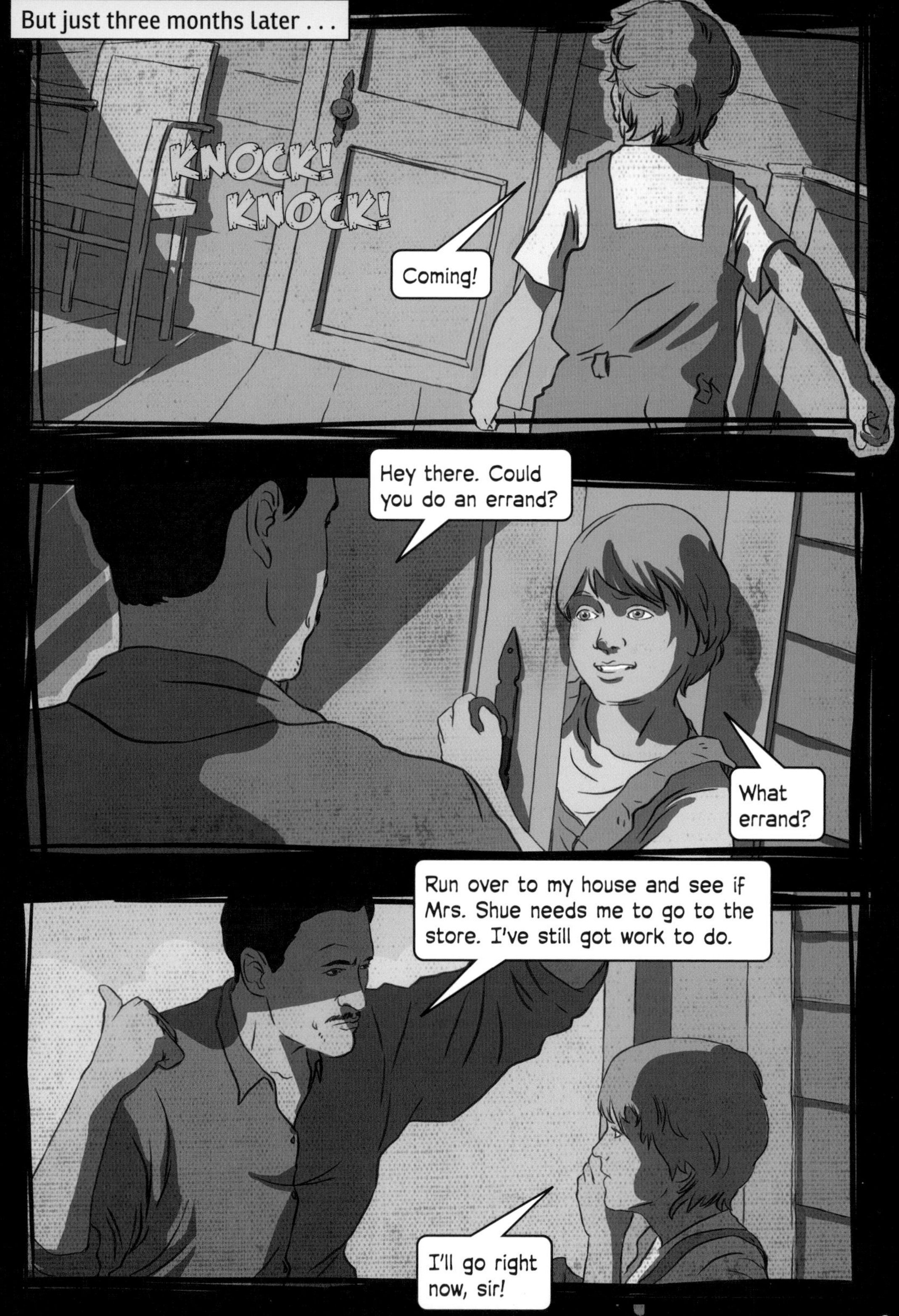

But just three months later . . .
KNOCK! KNOCK!
Coming!
Hey there. Could you do an errand?
What errand?
Run over to my house and see if Mrs. Shue needs me to go to the store. I've still got work to do.
I'll go right now, sir!

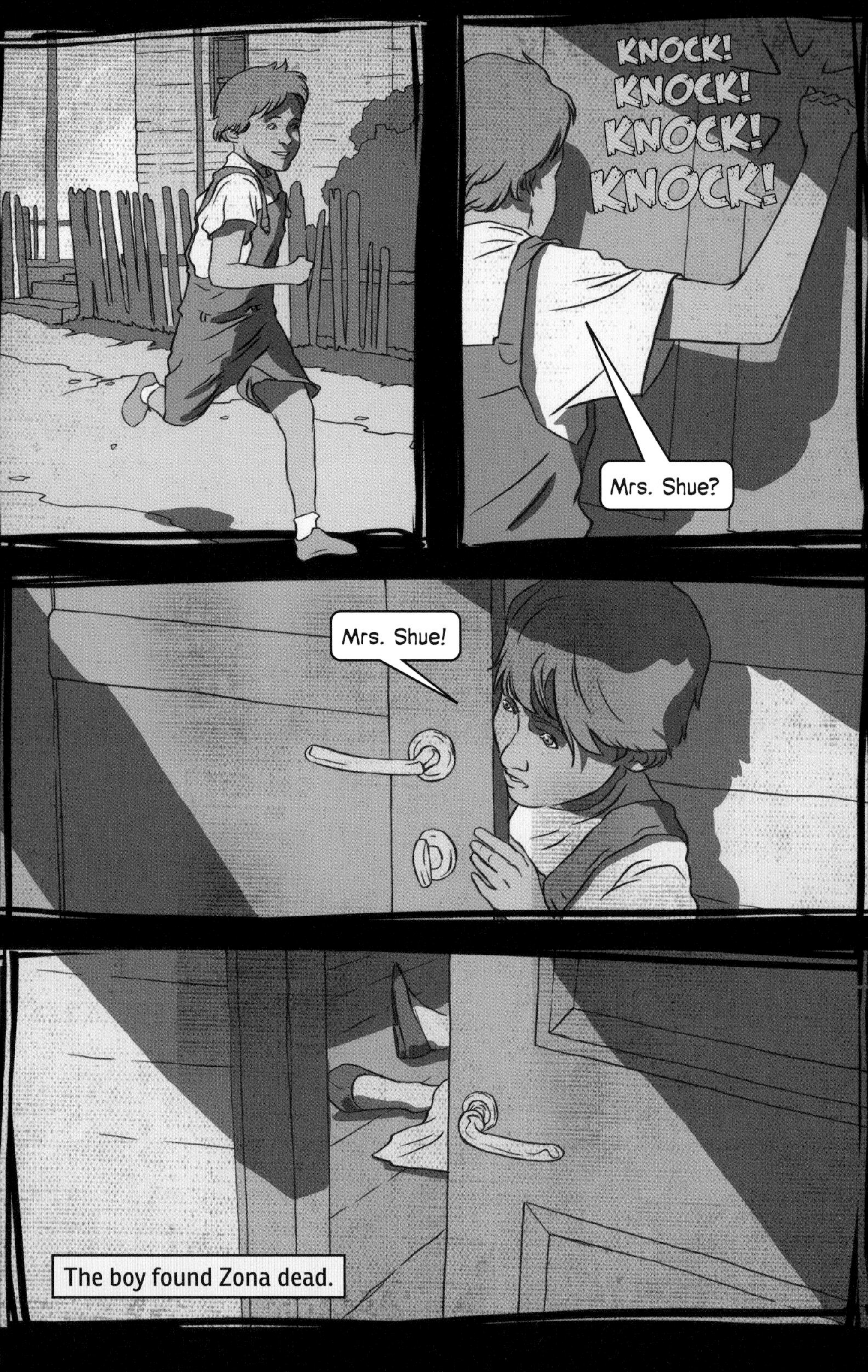
KNOCK! KNOCK! KNOCK! KNOCK!
Mrs. Shue?
Mrs. Shue!
The boy found Zona dead.

# CHAPTER 2
# THE HAUNTING OF MARY JANE

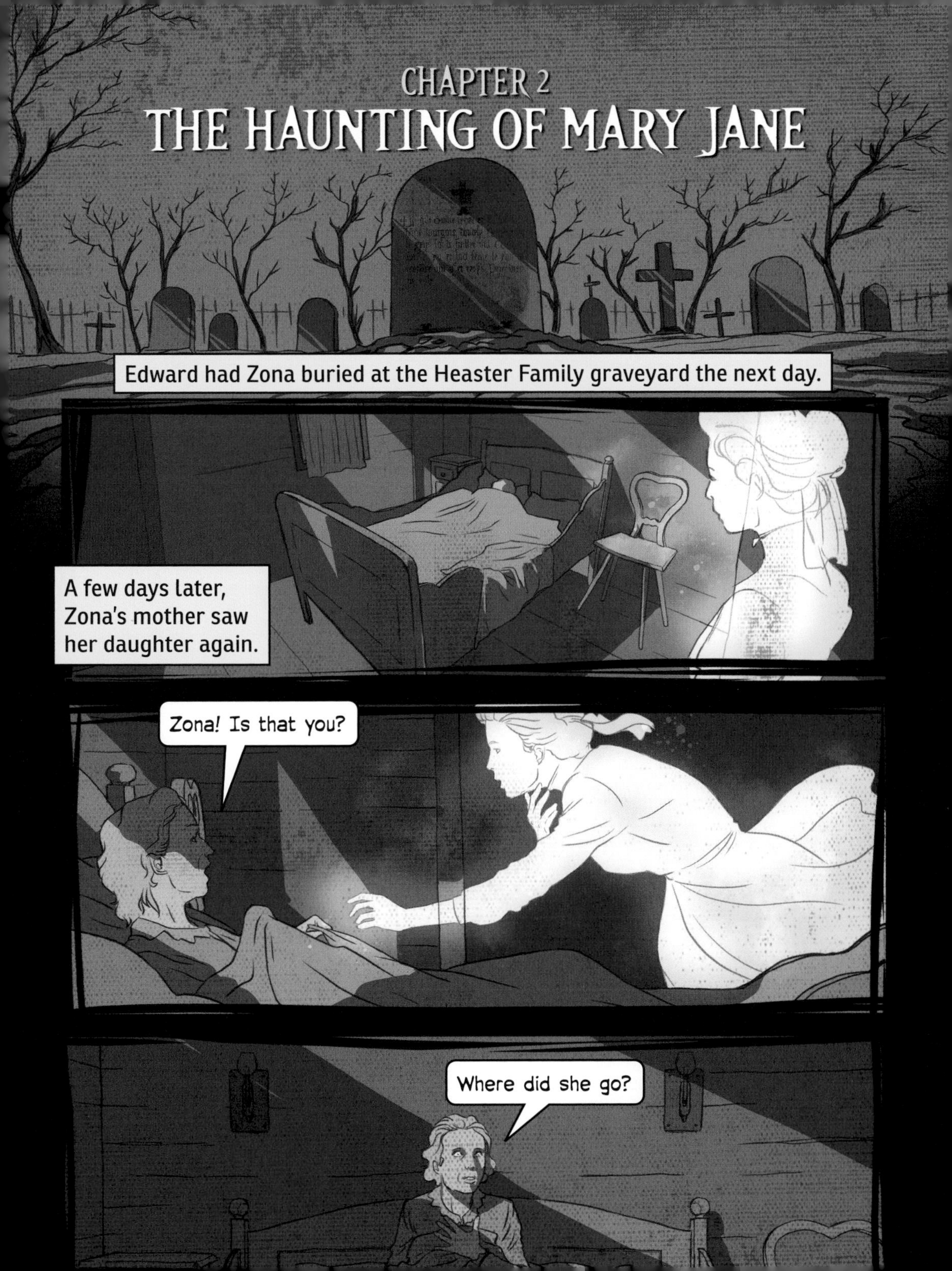
Edward had Zona buried at the Heaster Family graveyard the next day.
A few days later, Zona's mother saw her daughter again.
Zona! Is that you?
Where did she go?

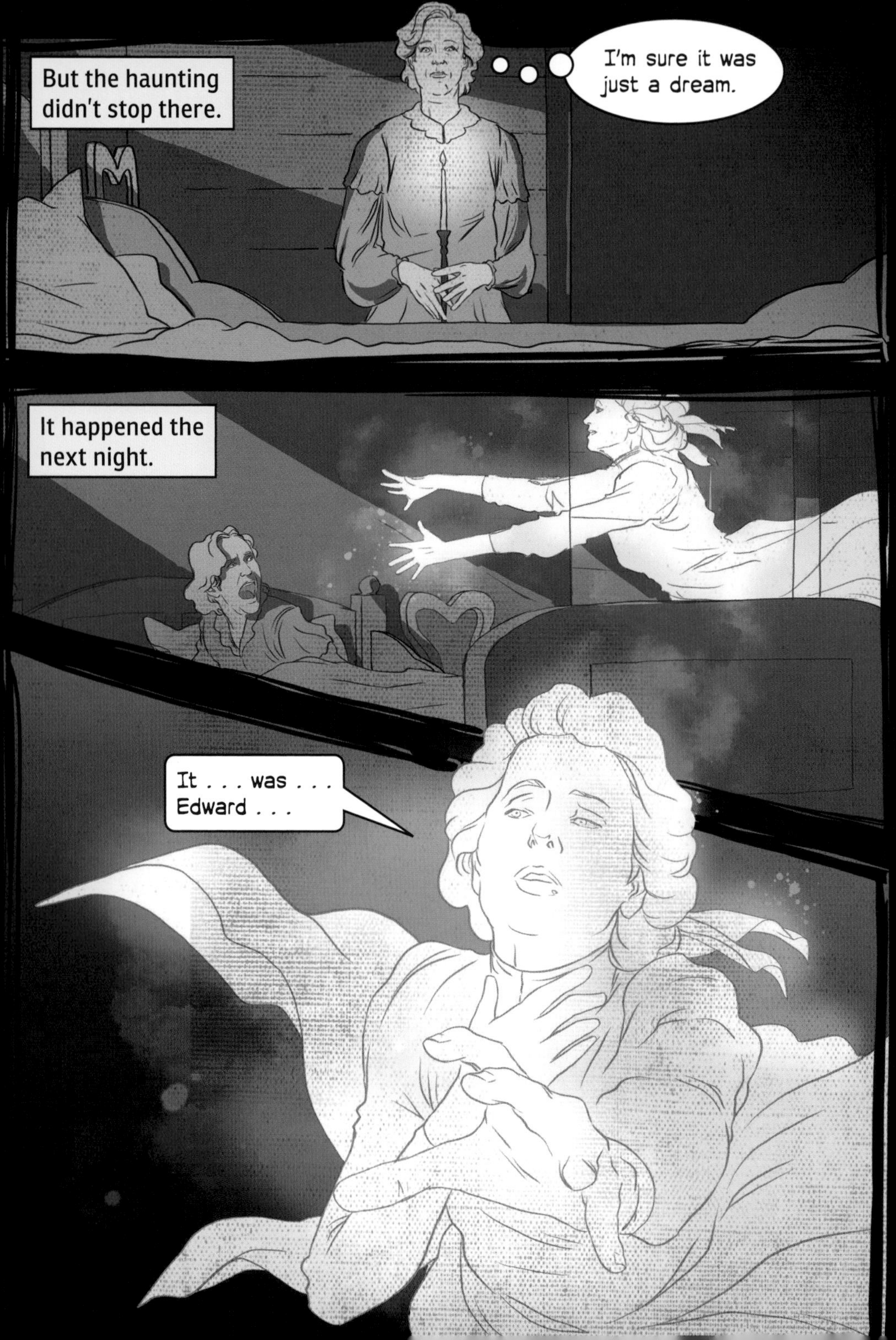
But the haunting didn't stop there.
I'm sure it was just a dream.
It happened the next night.
It . . . was . . . Edward . . .

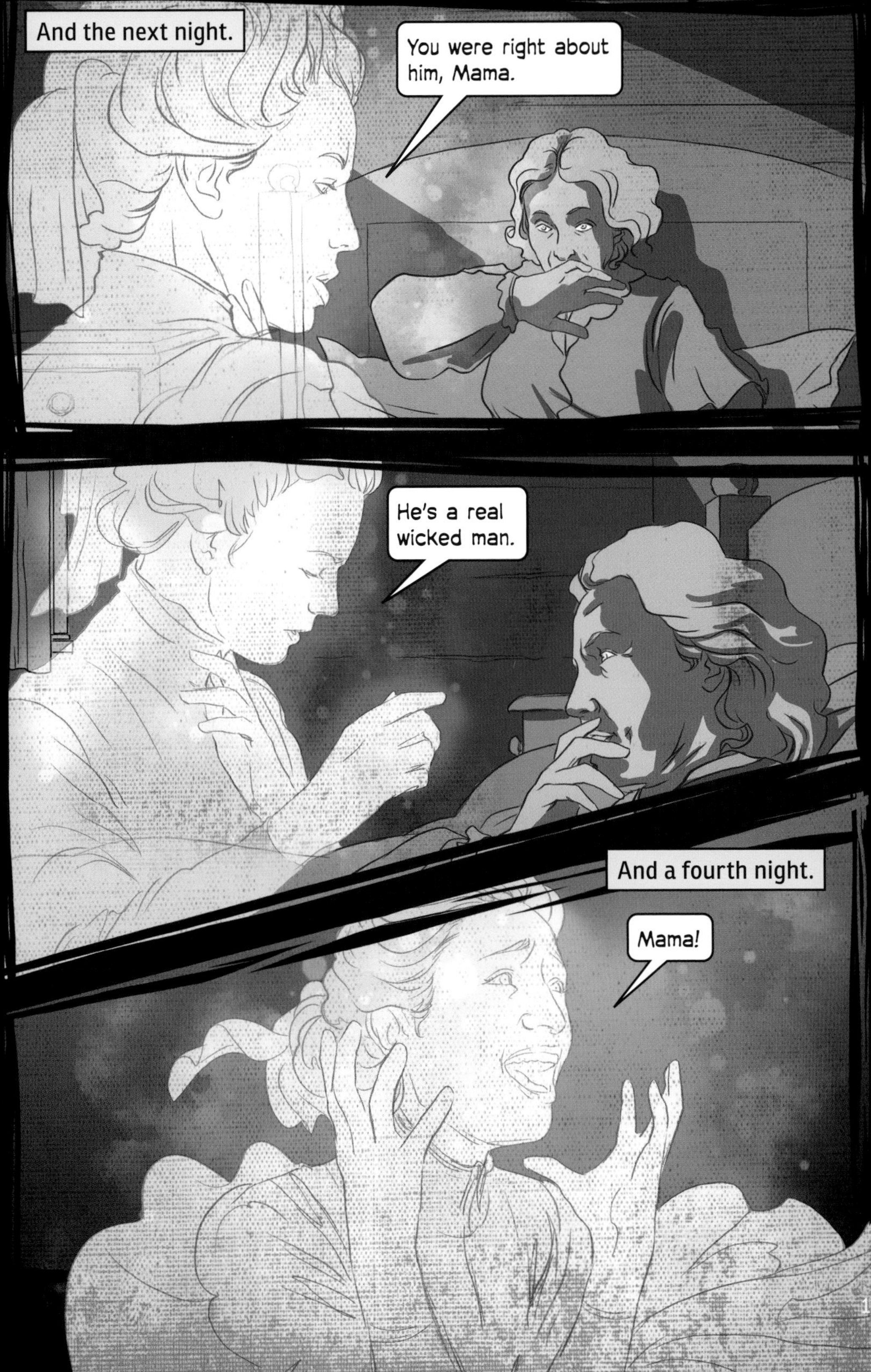
And the next night.
You were right about him, Mama.
He's a real wicked man.
And a fourth night.
Mama!

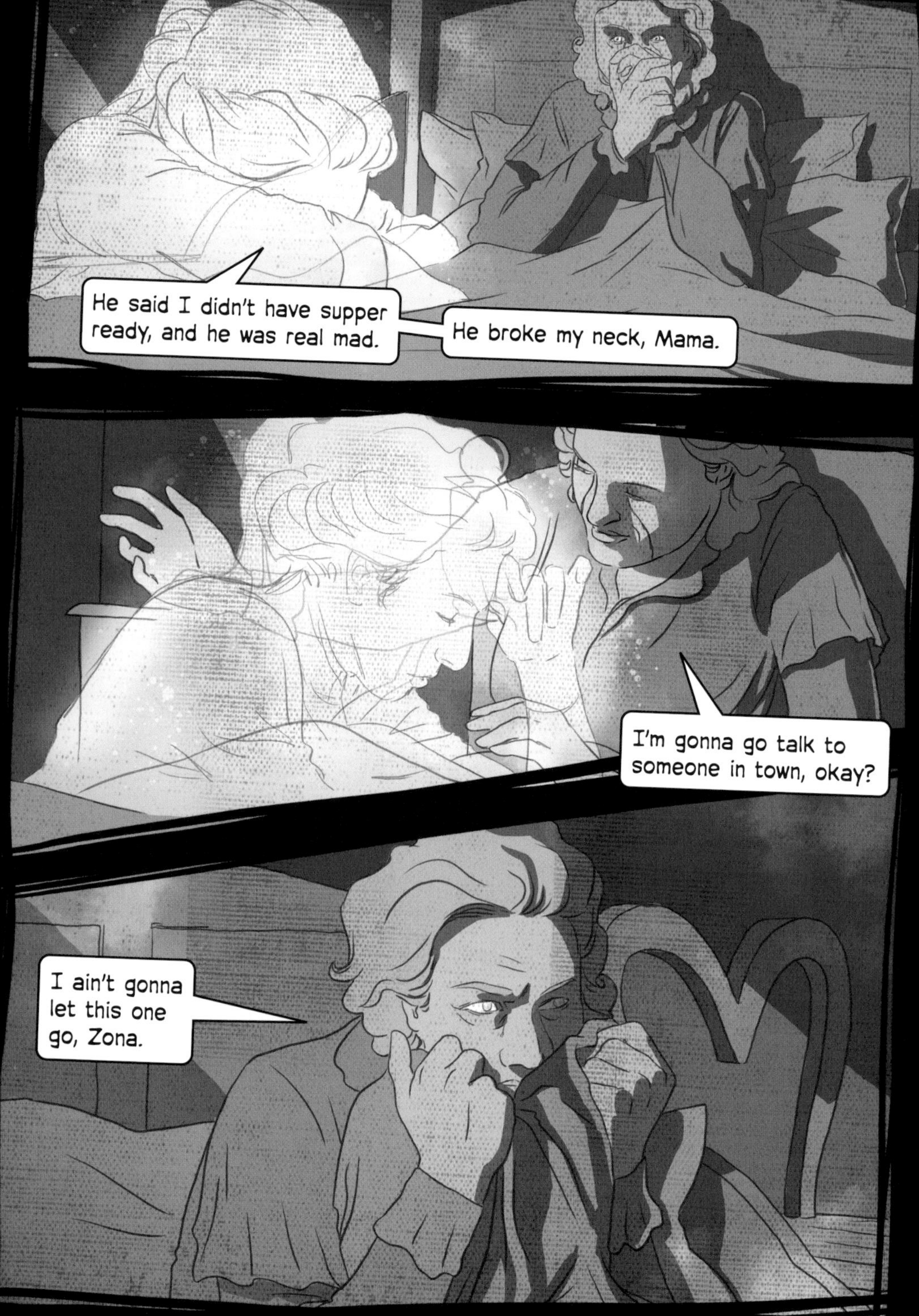
He said I didn't have supper ready, and he was real mad.
He broke my neck, Mama.
I'm gonna go talk to someone in town, okay?
I ain't gonna let this one go, Zona.

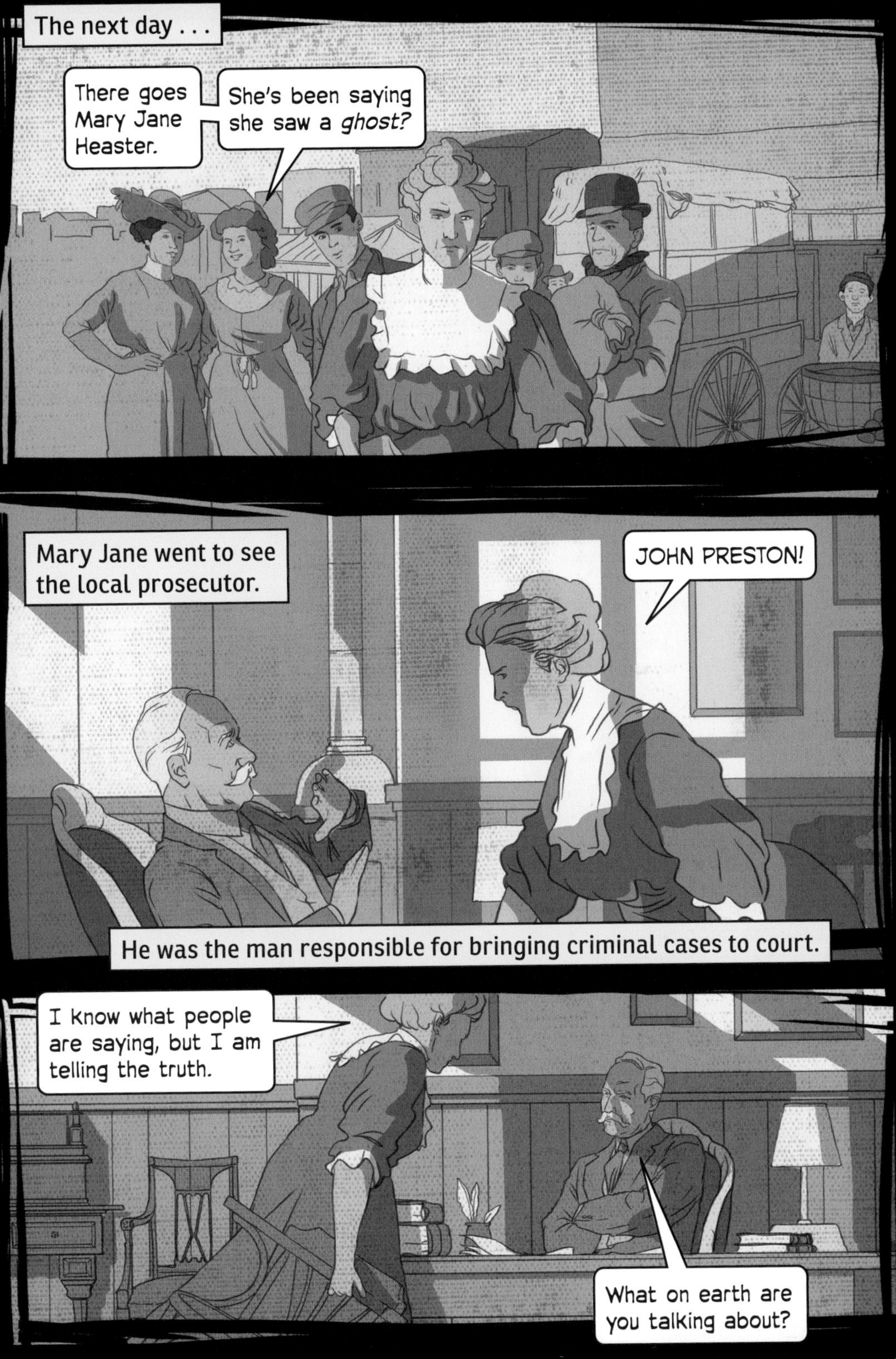
The next day . . .
There goes Mary Jane Heaster.
She's been saying she saw a *ghost?*
Mary Jane went to see the local prosecutor.
JOHN PRESTON!
He was the man responsible for bringing criminal cases to court.
I know what people are saying, but I am telling the truth.
What on earth are you talking about?

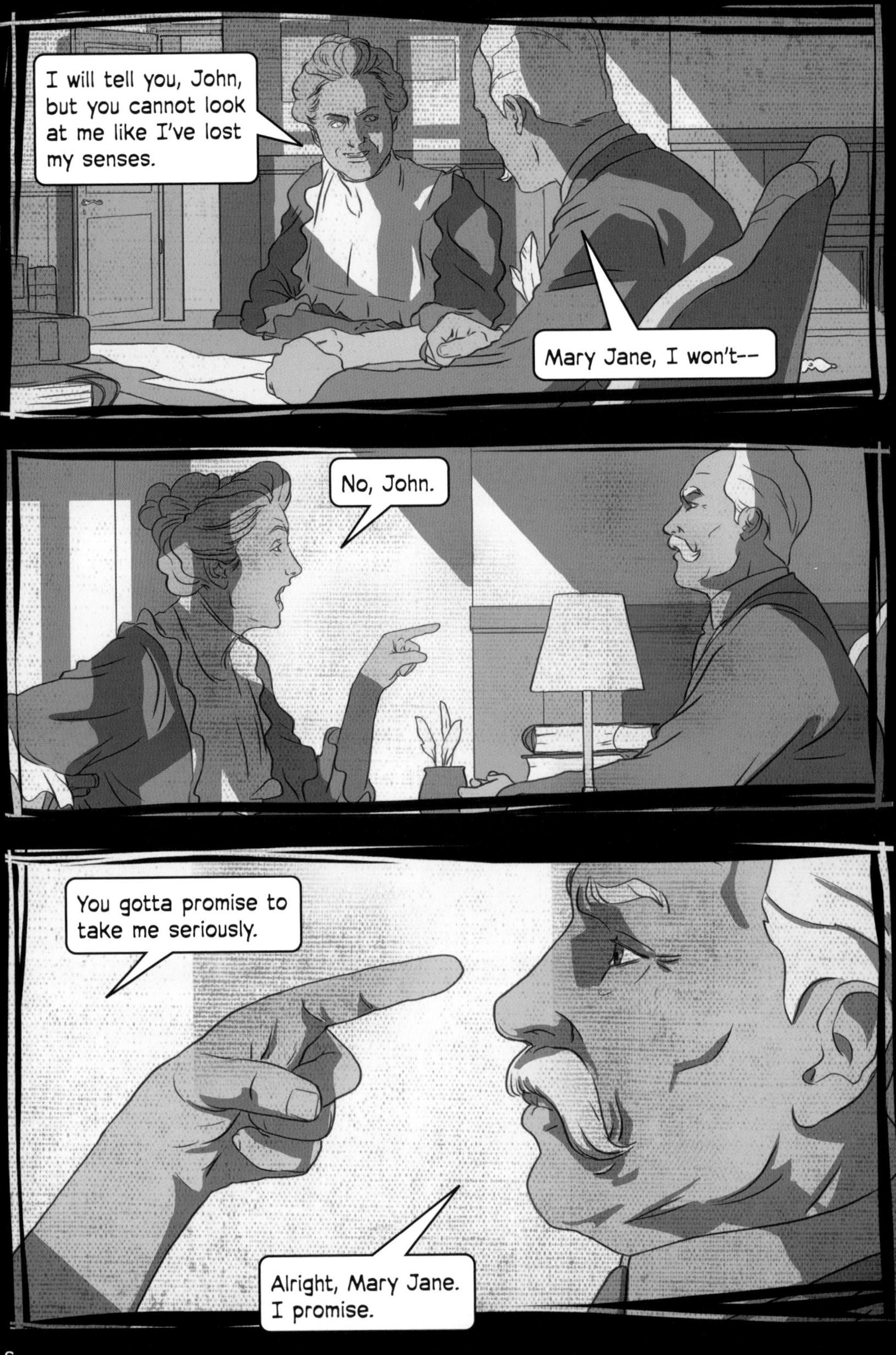
I will tell you, John, but you cannot look at me like I've lost my senses.
Mary Jane, I won't--
No, John.
You gotta promise to take me seriously.
Alright, Mary Jane. I promise.

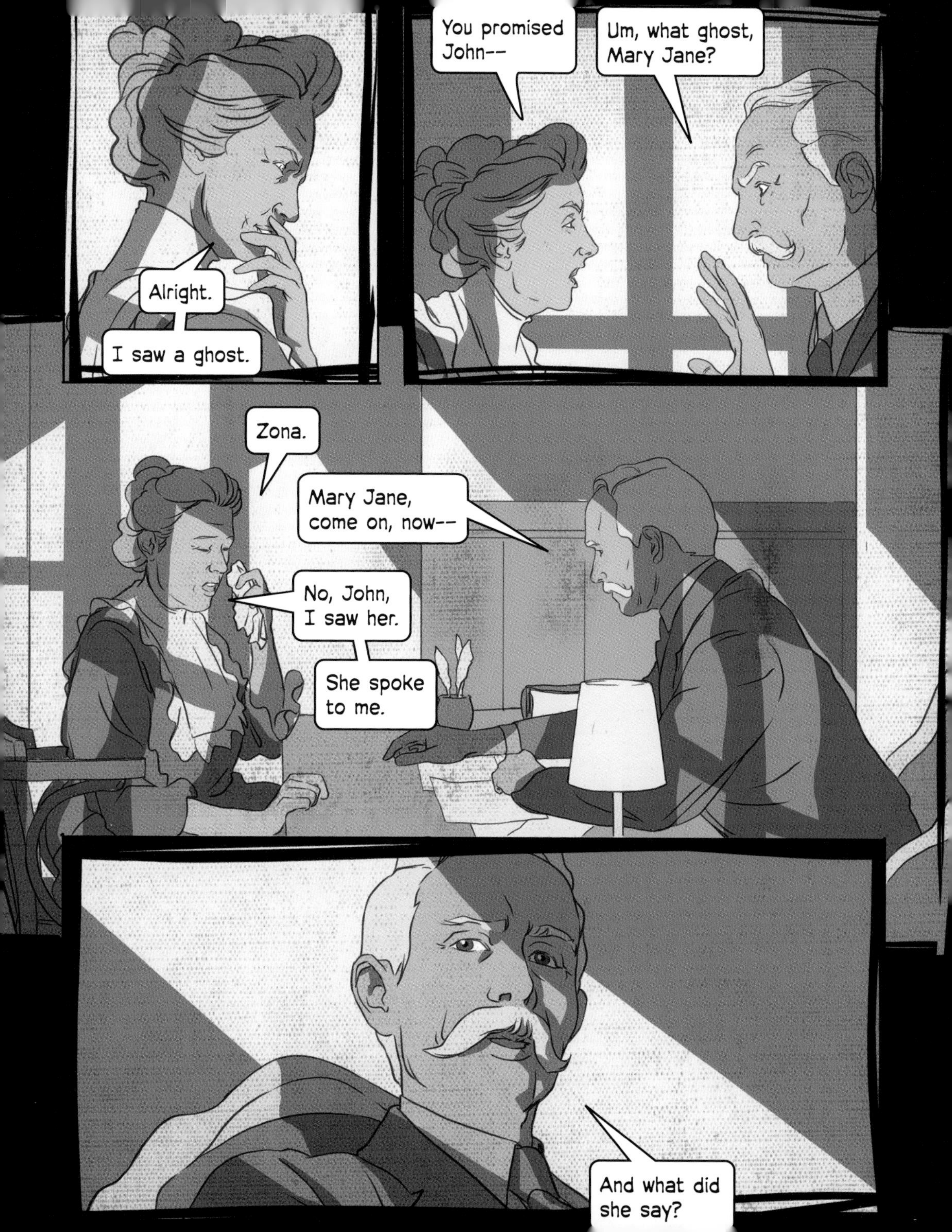
Alright.
I saw a ghost.
You promised John--
Um, what ghost, Mary Jane?
Zona.
Mary Jane, come on, now--
No, John, I saw her.
She spoke to me.
And what did she say?

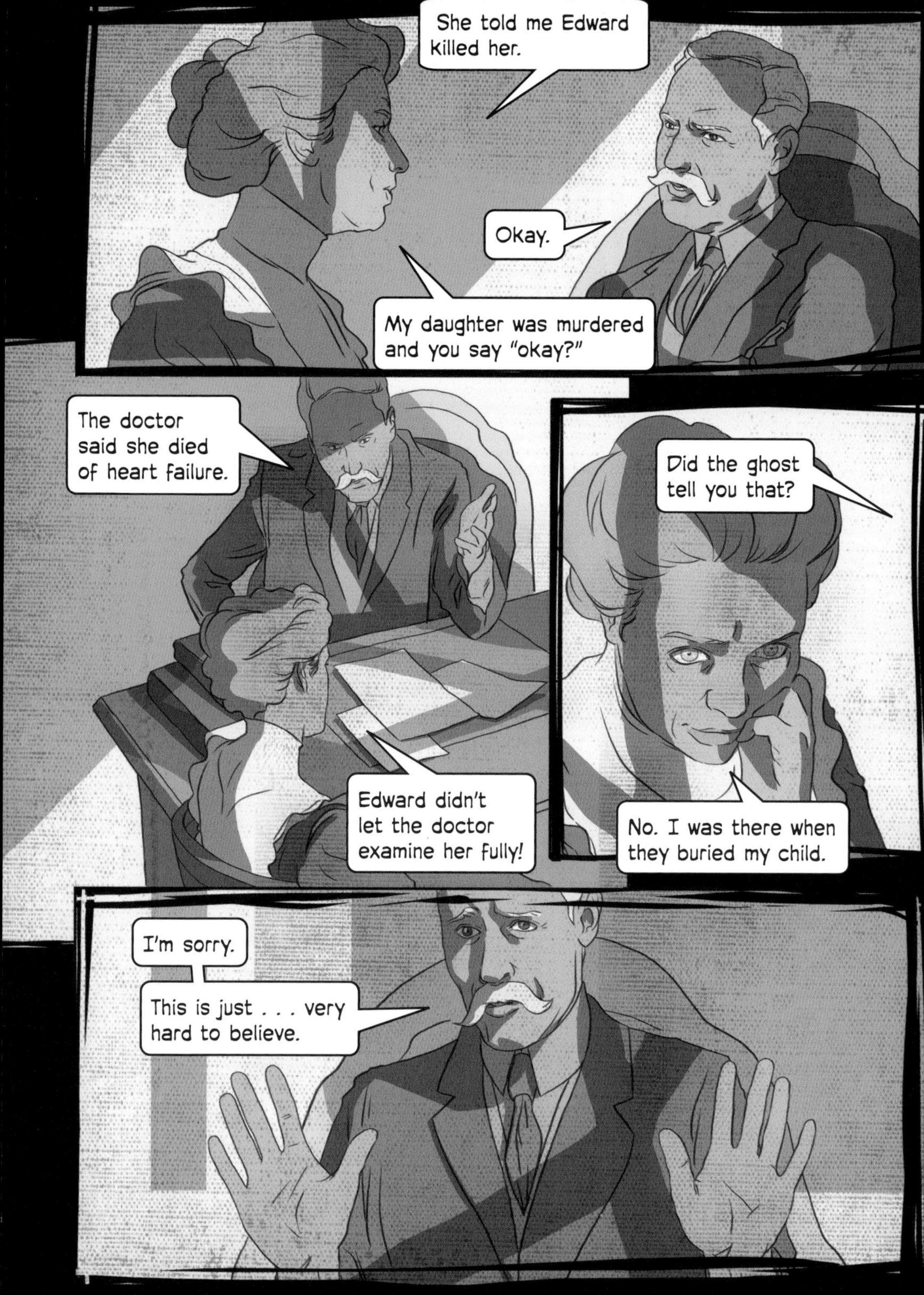
She told me Edward killed her.
Okay.
My daughter was murdered and you say "okay?"
The doctor said she died of heart failure.
Edward didn't let the doctor examine her fully!
Did the ghost tell you that?
No. I was there when they buried my child.
I'm sorry.
This is just . . . very hard to believe.

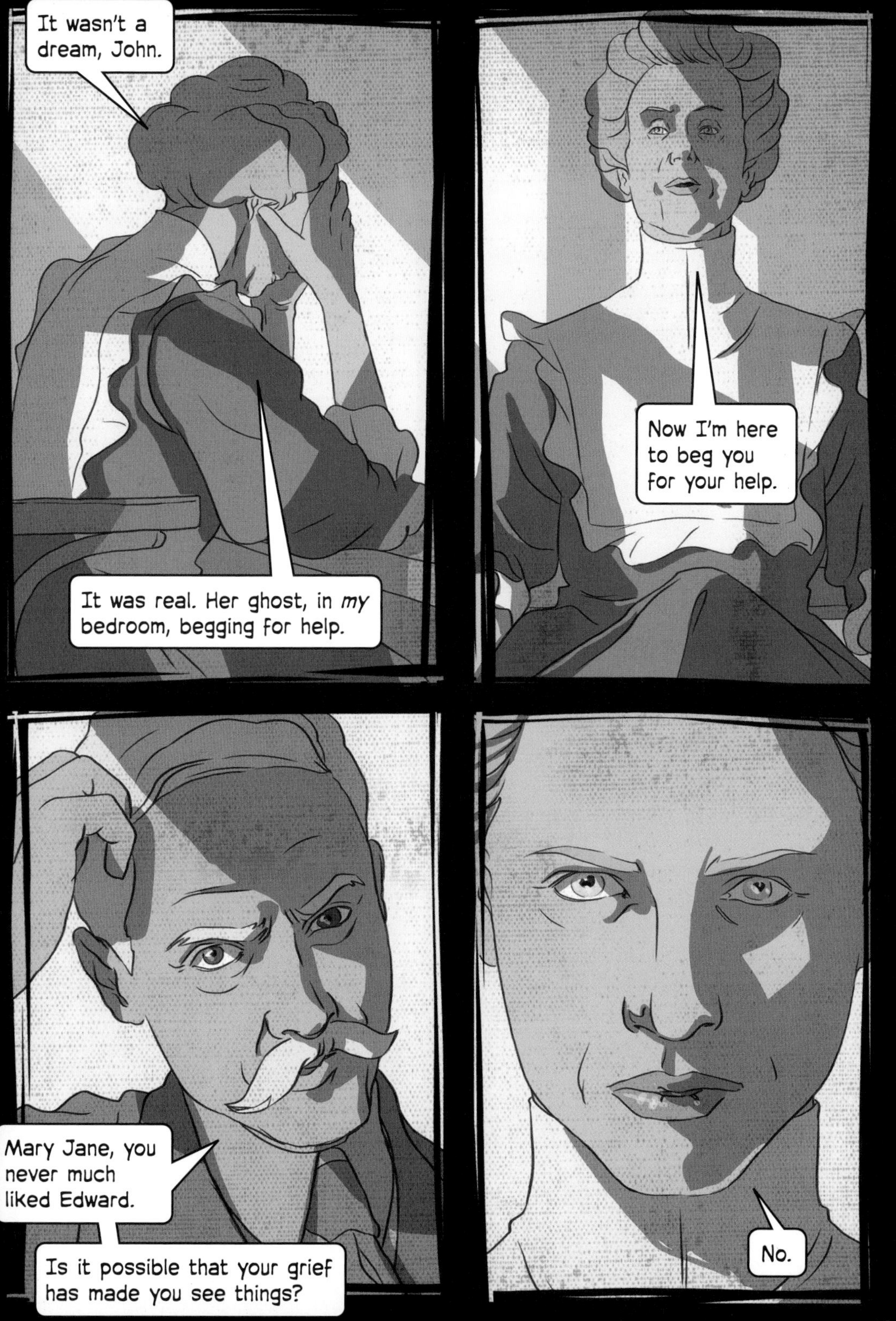
It wasn't a dream, John.
It was real. Her ghost, in *my* bedroom, begging for help.
Now I'm here to beg you for your help.
Mary Jane, you never much liked Edward.
Is it possible that your grief has made you see things?
No.

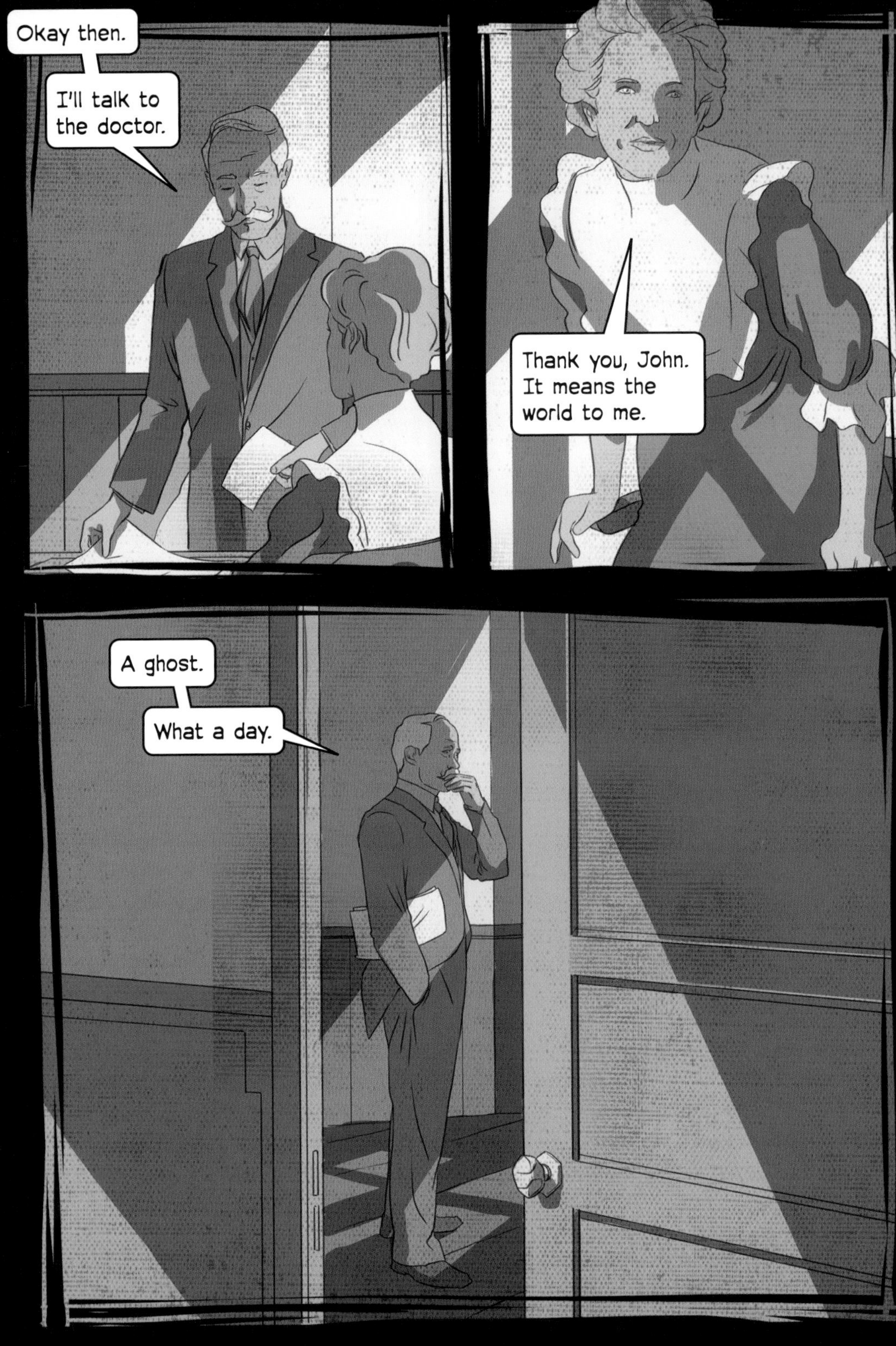
Okay then.
I'll talk to the doctor.
Thank you, John. It means the world to me.
A ghost.
What a day.

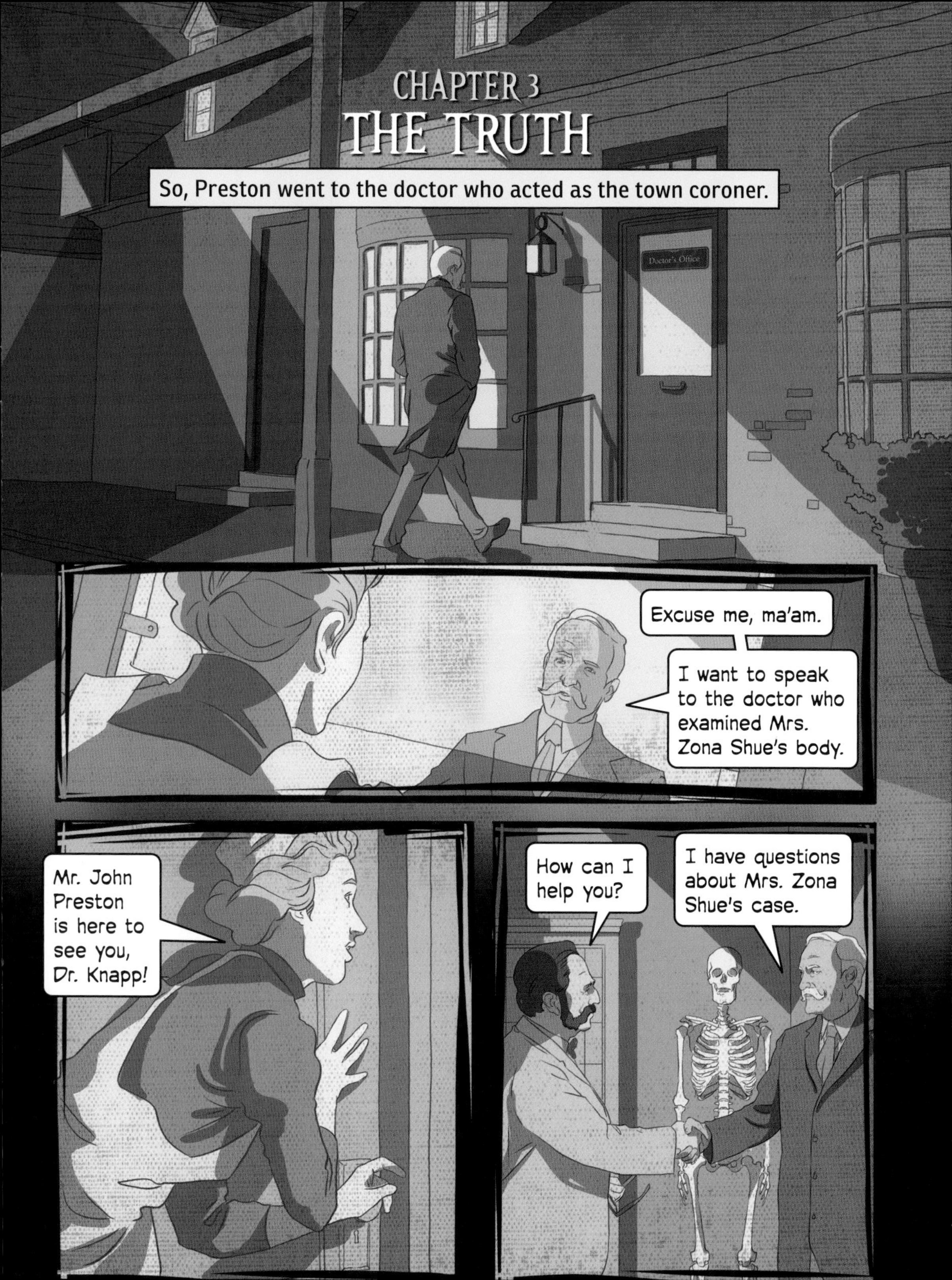
CHAPTER 3
THE TRUTH
So, Preston went to the doctor who acted as the town coroner.
Doctor's Office
Excuse me, ma'am.
I want to speak to the doctor who examined Mrs. Zona Shue's body.
Mr. John Preston is here to see you, Dr. Knapp!
How can I help you?
I have questions about Mrs. Zona Shue's case.

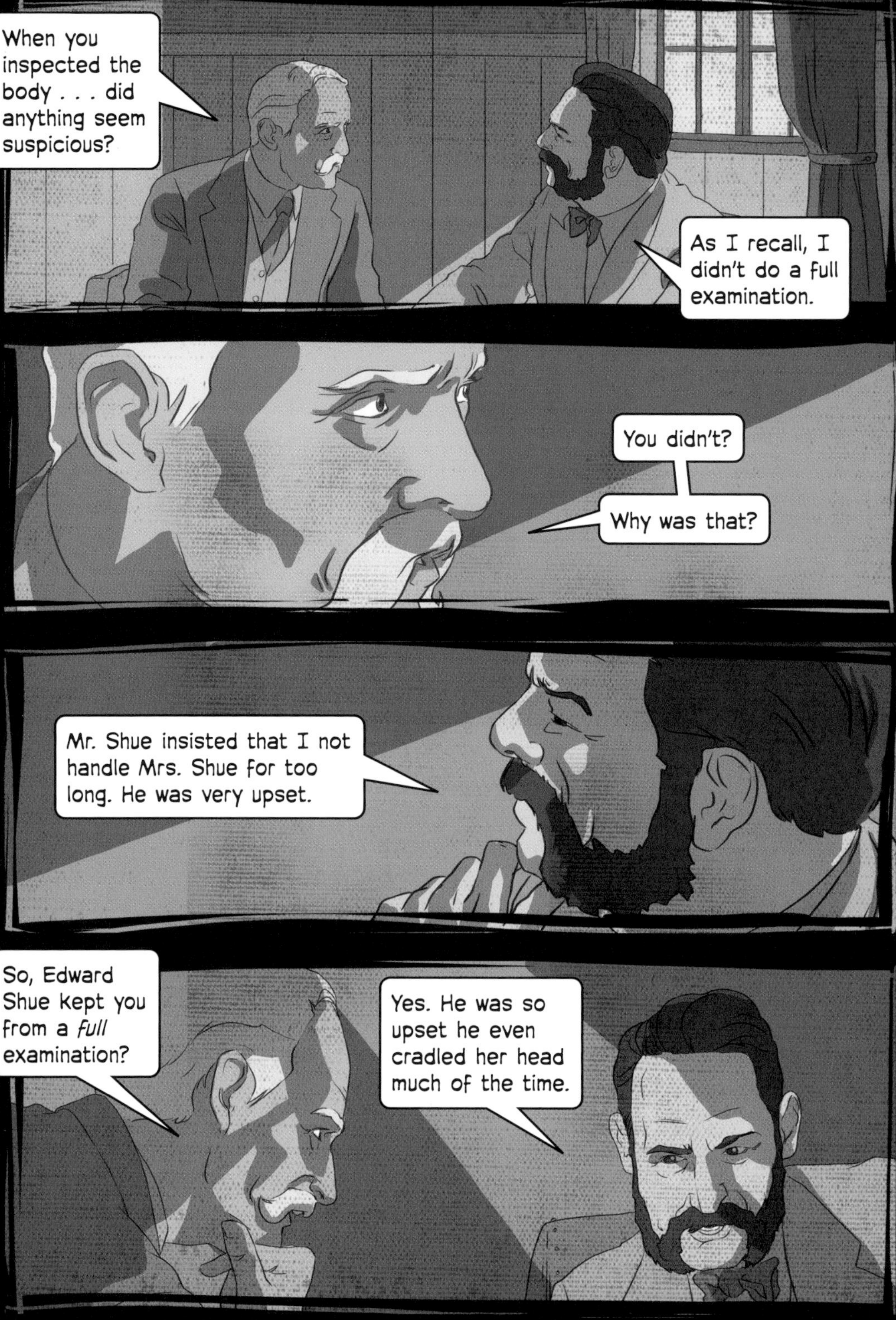
When you inspected the body . . . did anything seem suspicious?
As I recall, I didn't do a full examination.
You didn't?
Why was that?
Mr. Shue insisted that I not handle Mrs. Shue for too long. He was very upset.
So, Edward Shue kept you from a *full* examination?
Yes. He was so upset he even cradled her head much of the time.

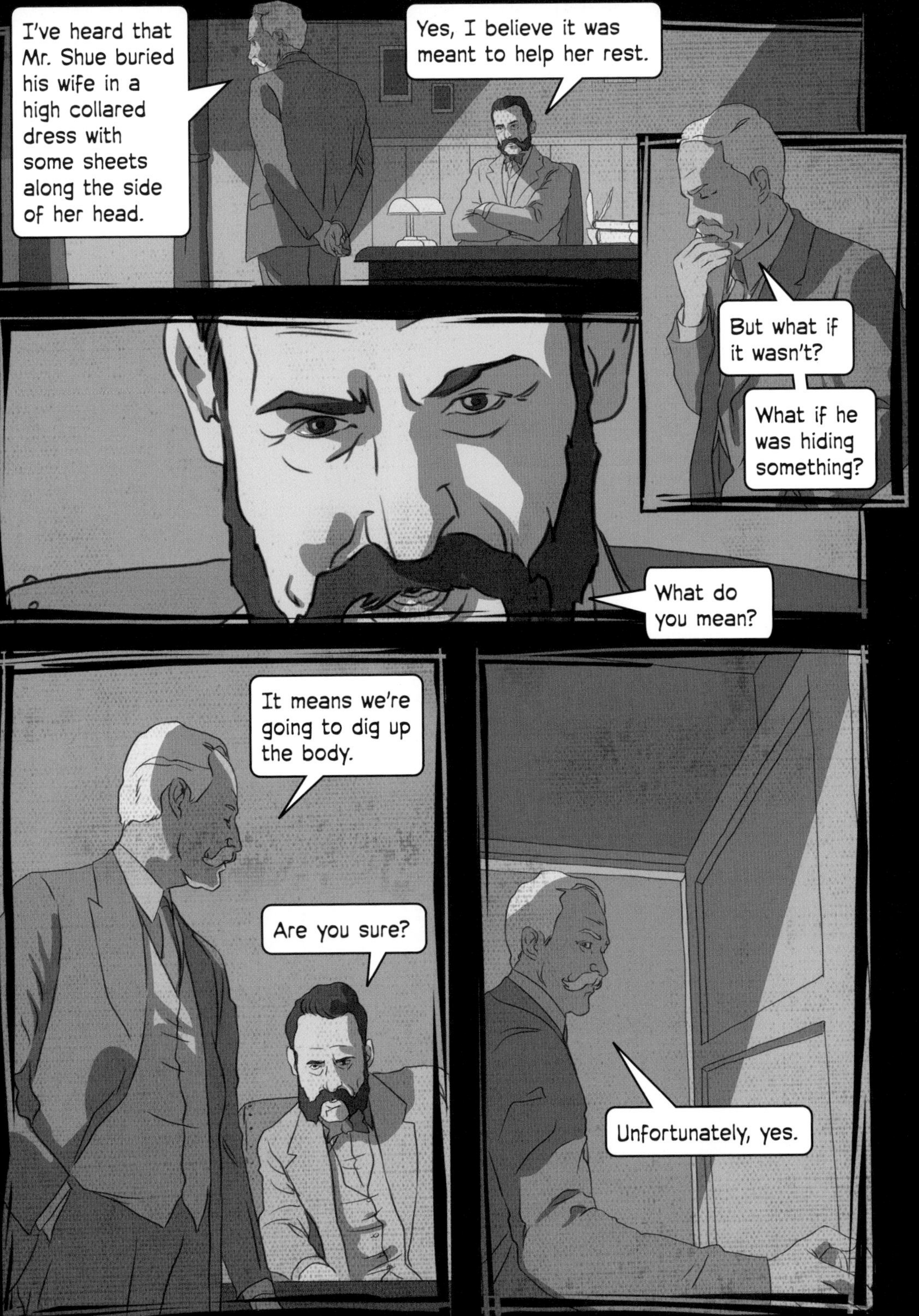
I've heard that Mr. Shue buried his wife in a high collared dress with some sheets along the side of her head.
Yes, I believe it was meant to help her rest.
But what if it wasn't?
What if he was hiding something?
What do you mean?
It means we're going to dig up the body.
Are you sure?
Unfortunately, yes.

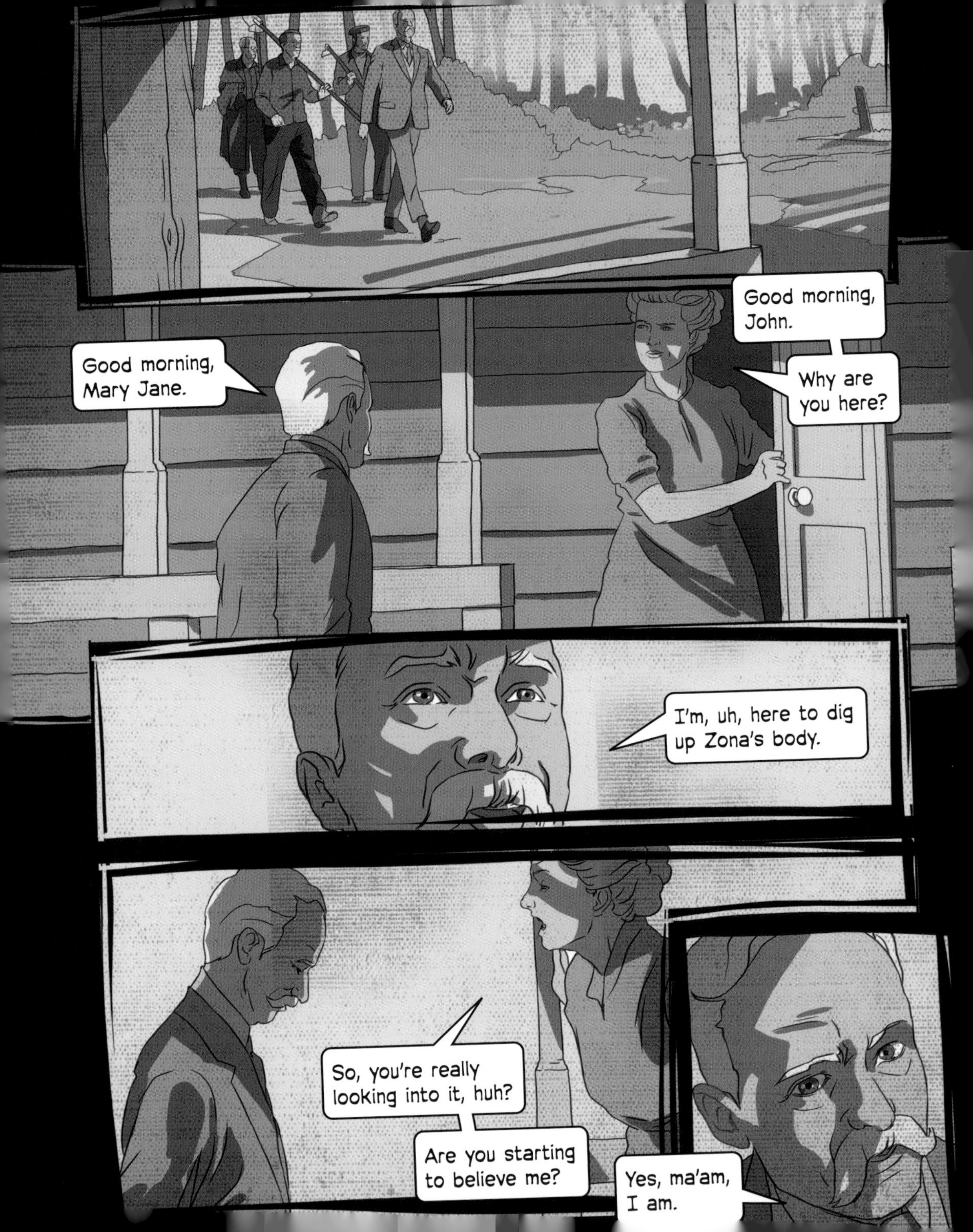
Good morning, John.
Why are you here?
Good morning, Mary Jane.
I'm, uh, here to dig up Zona's body.
So, you're really looking into it, huh?
Are you starting to believe me?
Yes, ma'am, I am.

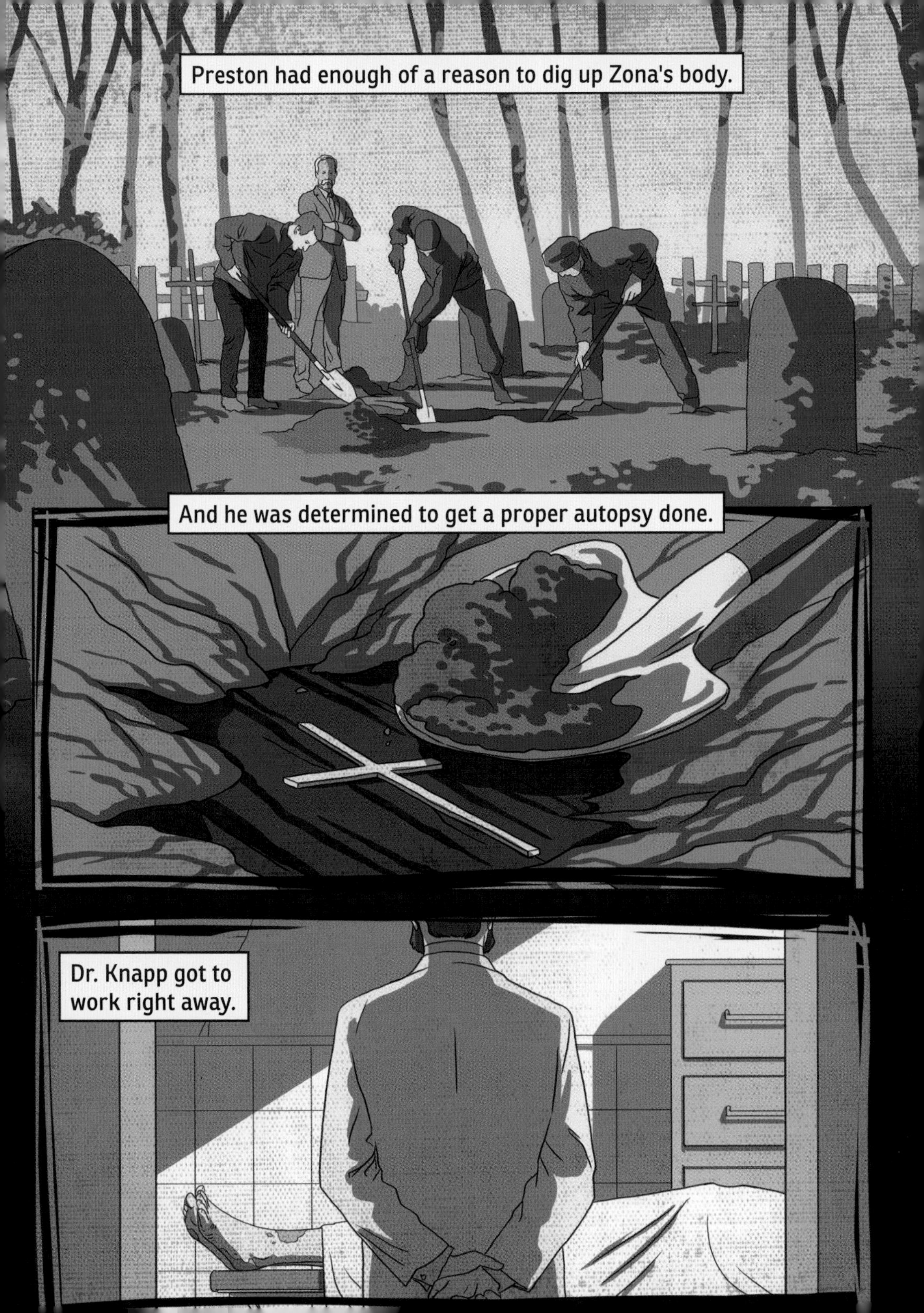
Preston had enough of a reason to dig up Zona's body.
And he was determined to get a proper autopsy done.
Dr. Knapp got to work right away.

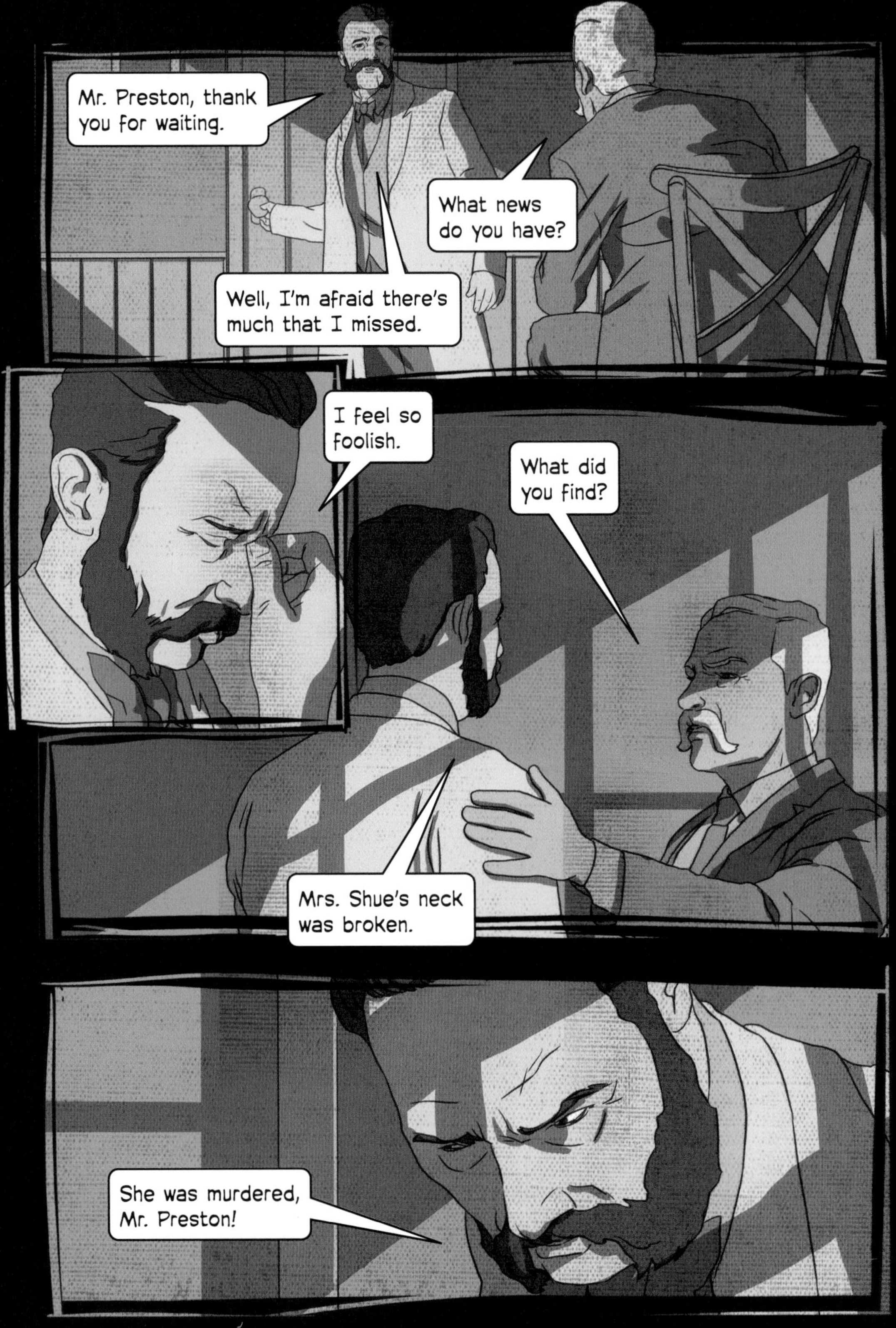
Mr. Preston, thank you for waiting.
What news do you have?
Well, I'm afraid there's much that I missed.
I feel so foolish.
What did you find?
Mrs. Shue's neck was broken.
She was murdered, Mr. Preston!

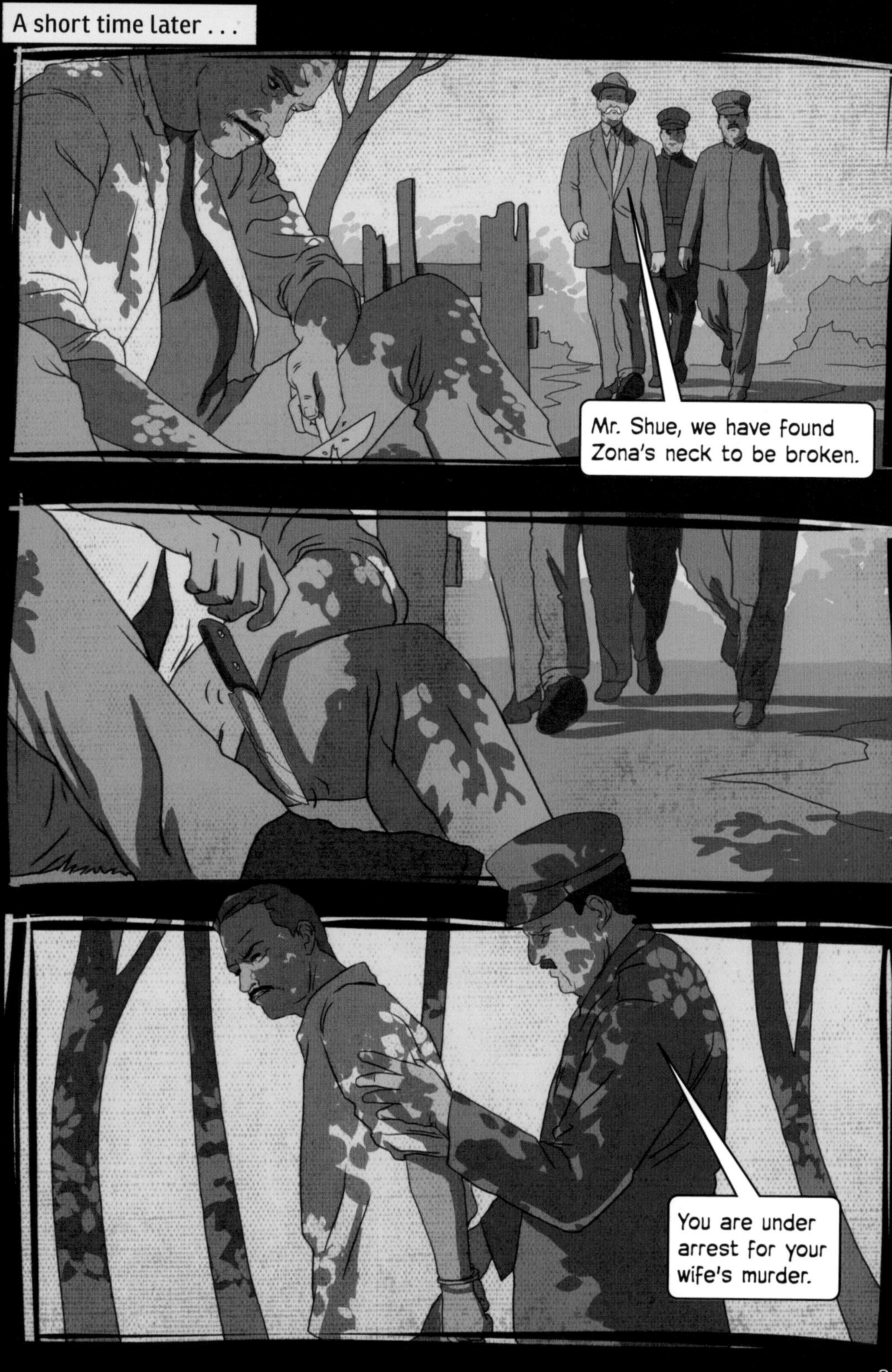
A short time later . . .
Mr. Shue, we have found Zona's neck to be broken.
You are under arrest for your wife's murder.

# CHAPTER 4
# THE TRIAL OF EDWARD SHUE

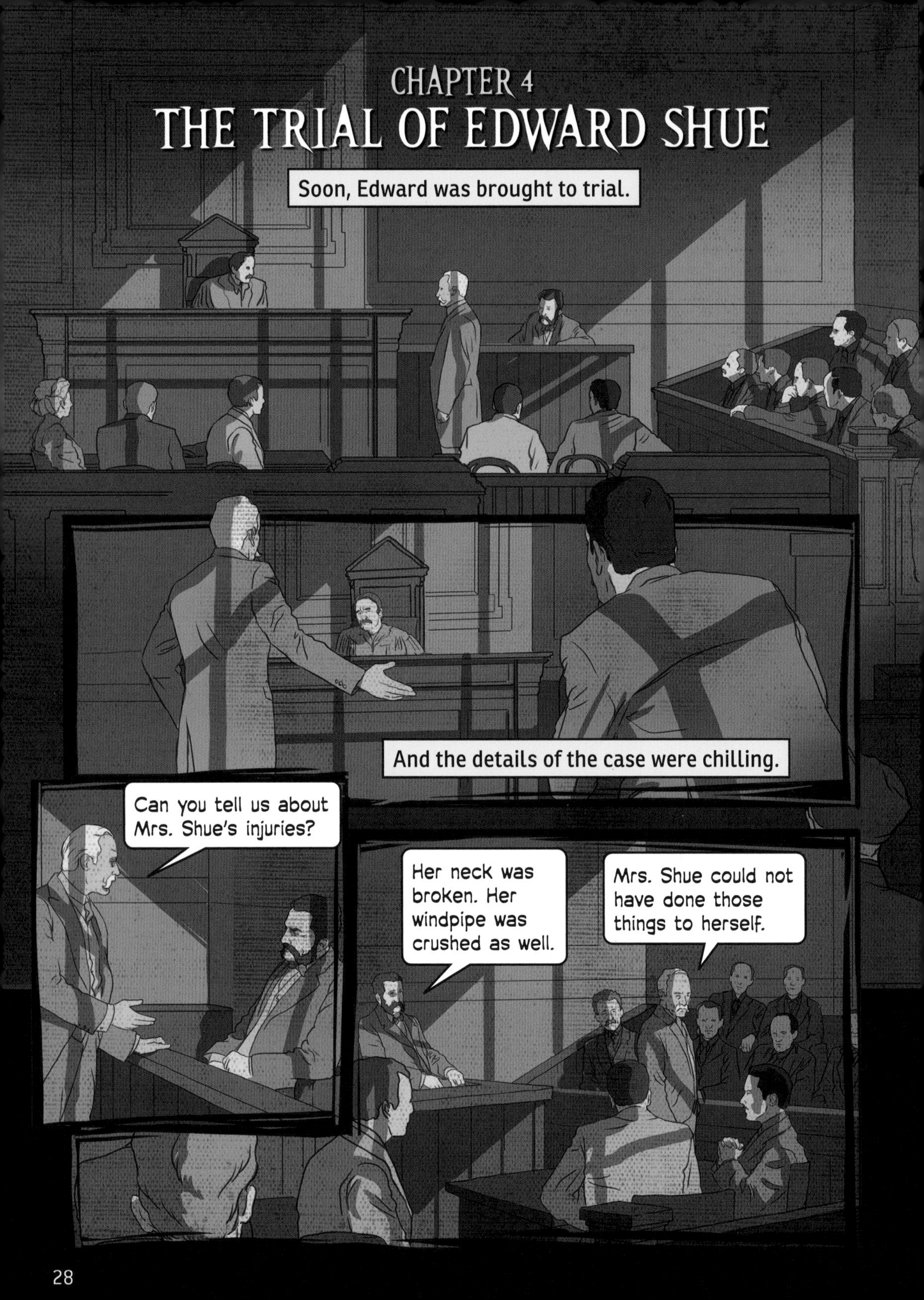

Soon, Edward was brought to trial.
And the details of the case were chilling.
Can you tell us about Mrs. Shue's injuries?
Her neck was broken. Her windpipe was crushed as well.
Mrs. Shue could not have done those things to herself.

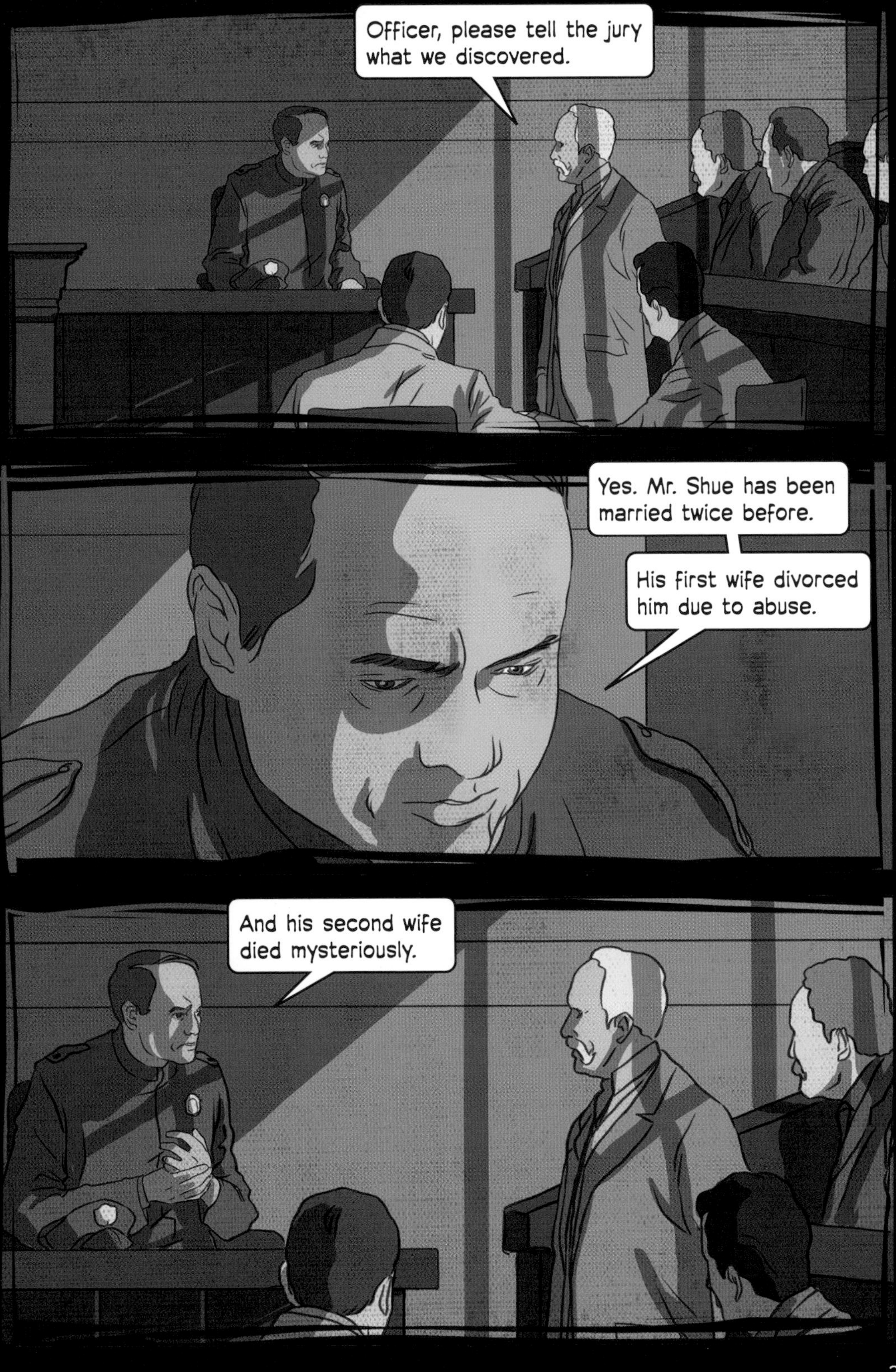
Officer, please tell the jury what we discovered.
Yes. Mr. Shue has been married twice before.
His first wife divorced him due to abuse.
And his second wife died mysteriously.

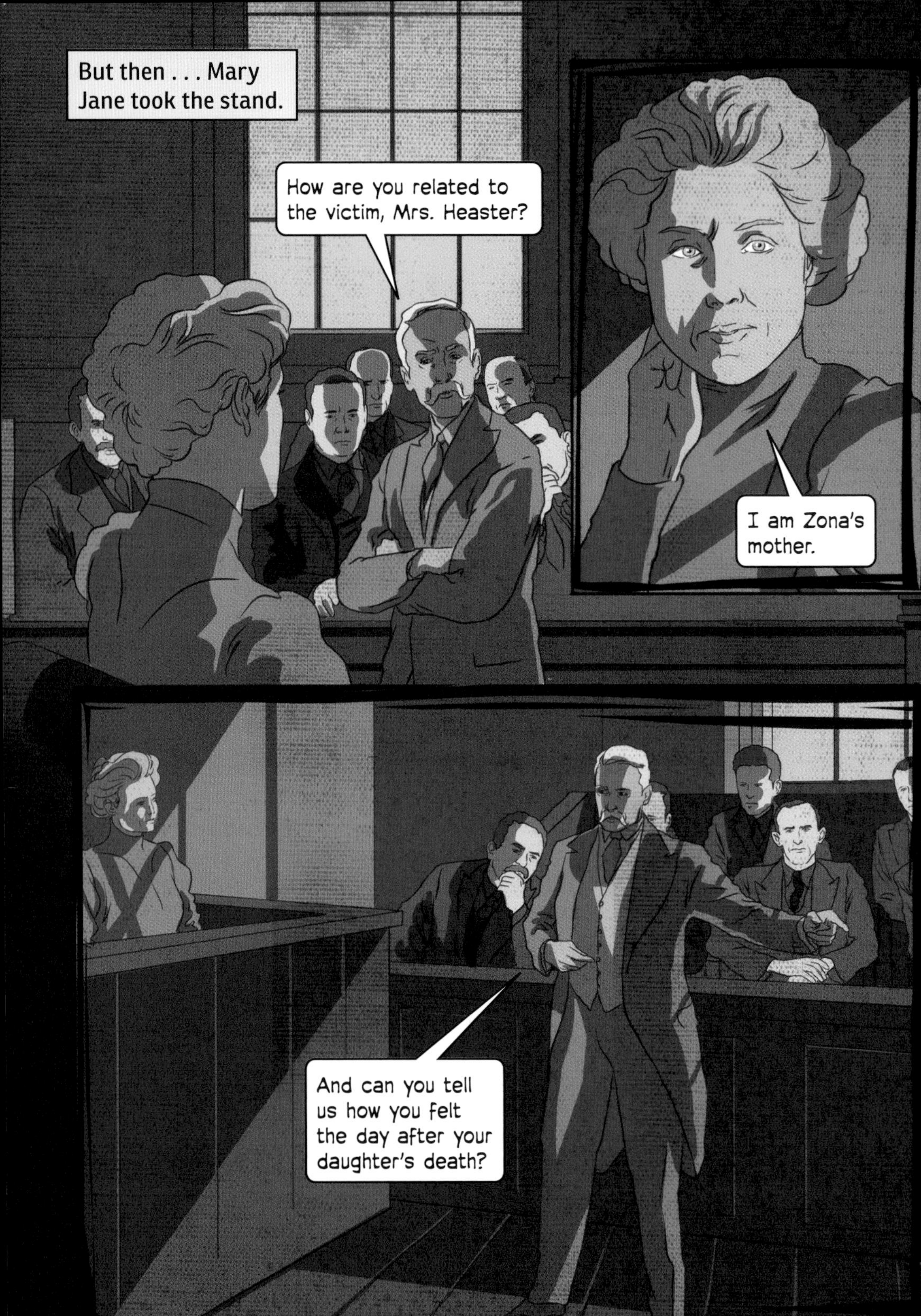
But then . . . Mary Jane took the stand.
How are you related to the victim, Mrs. Heaster?
I am Zona's mother.
And can you tell us how you felt the day after your daughter's death?

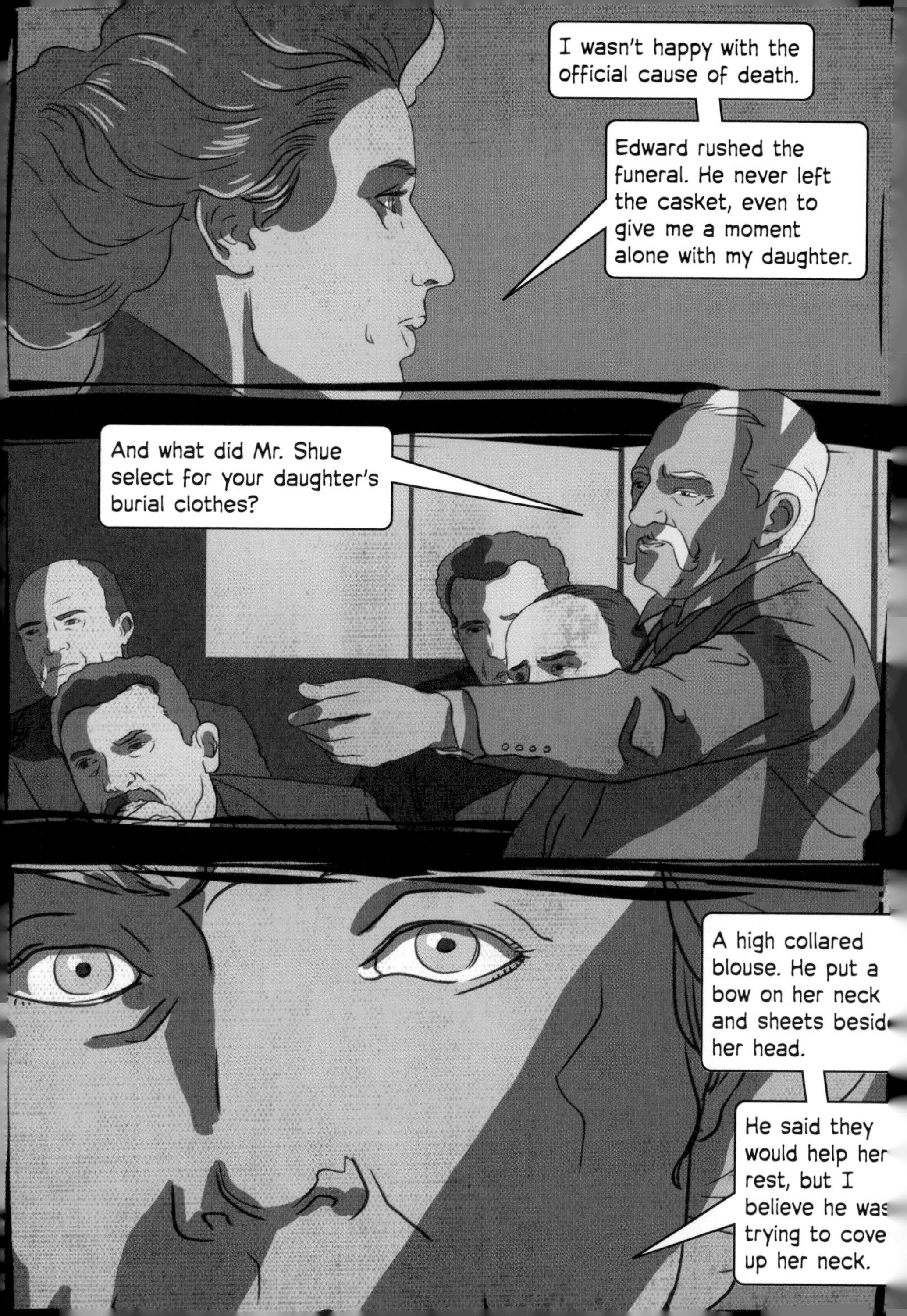
I wasn't happy with the official cause of death.
Edward rushed the funeral. He never left the casket, even to give me a moment alone with my daughter.
And what did Mr. Shue select for your daughter's burial clothes?
A high collared blouse. He put a bow on her neck and sheets besid her head.
He said they would help her rest, but I believe he was trying to cove up her neck.

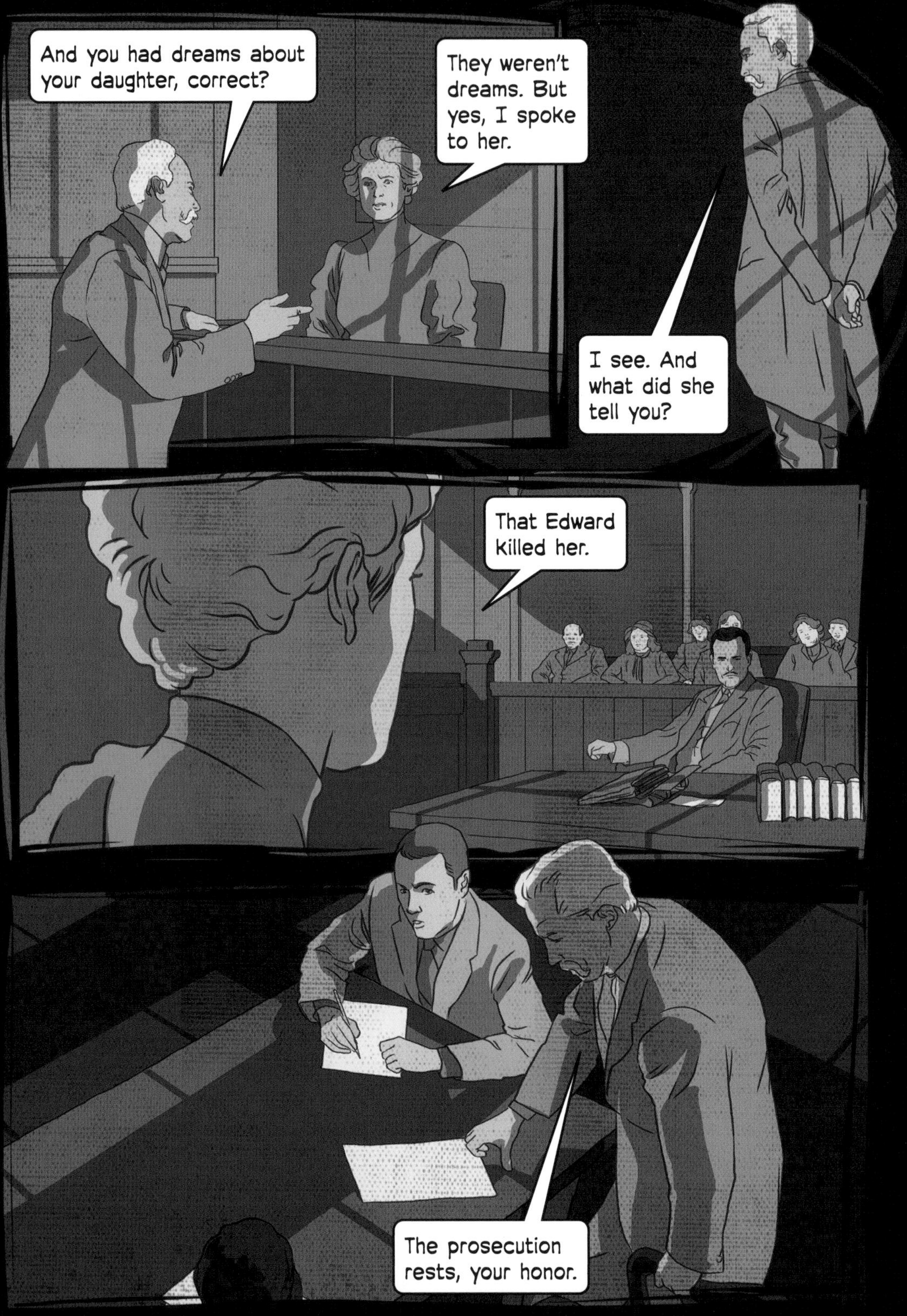
And you had dreams about your daughter, correct?
They weren't dreams. But yes, I spoke to her.
I see. And what did she tell you?
That Edward killed her.
The prosecution rests, your honor.

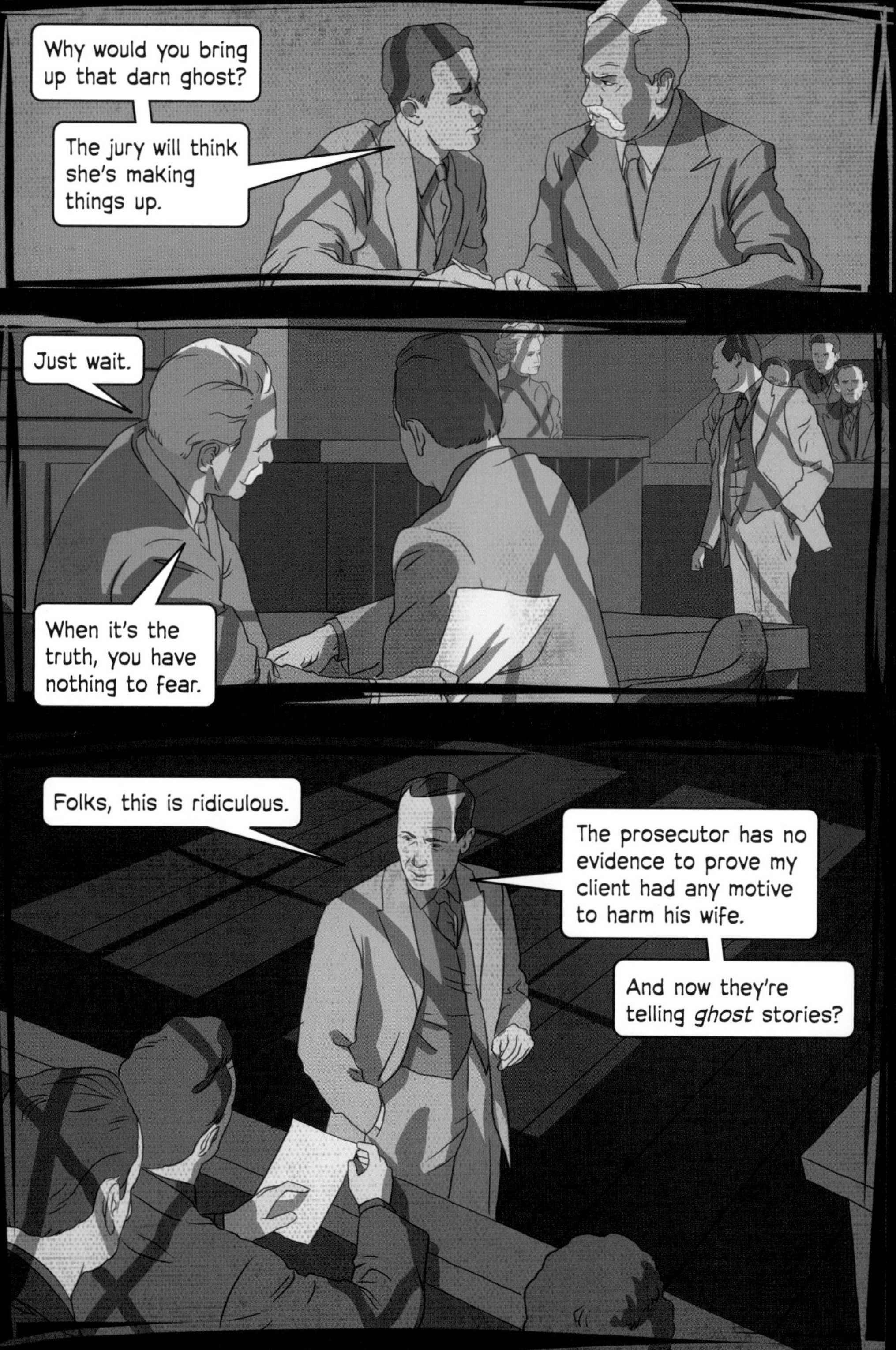
Why would you bring up that darn ghost?
The jury will think she's making things up.
Just wait.
When it's the truth, you have nothing to fear.
Folks, this is ridiculous.
The prosecutor has no evidence to prove my client had any motive to harm his wife.
And now they're telling *ghost* stories?

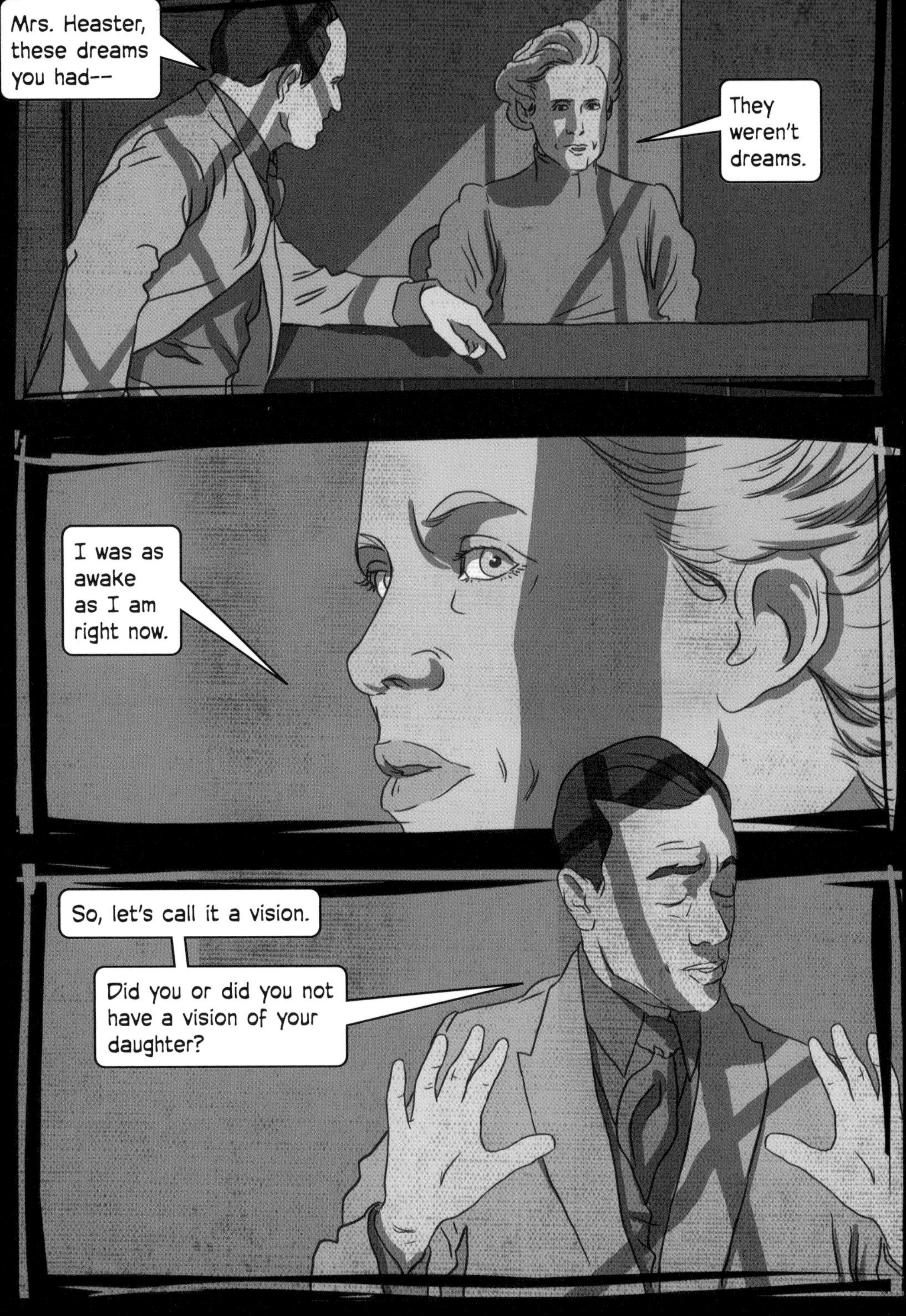
Mrs. Heaster, these dreams you had--
They weren't dreams.
I was as awake as I am right now.
So, let's call it a vision.
Did you or did you not have a vision of your daughter?

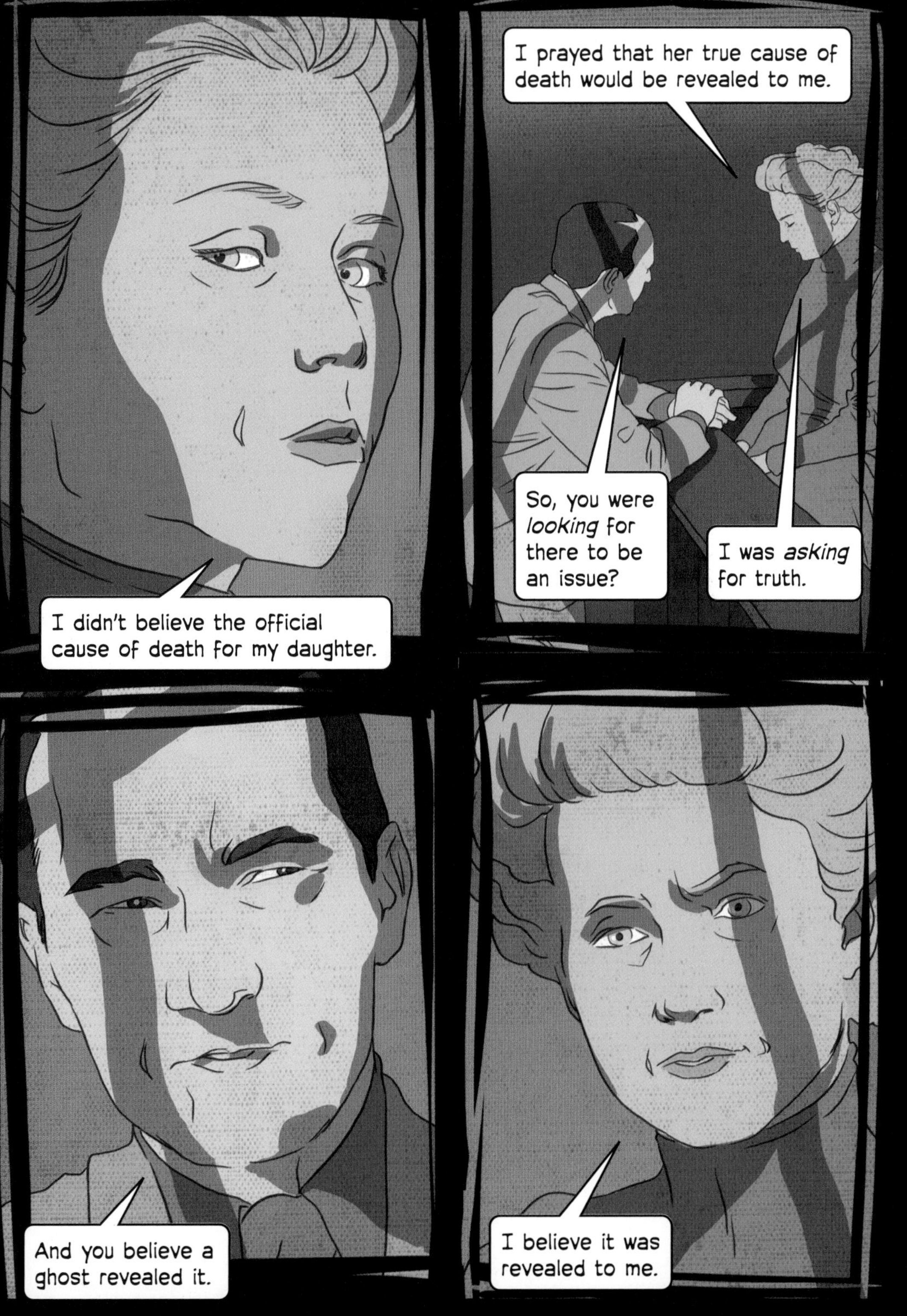
I didn't believe the official cause of death for my daughter.
I prayed that her true cause of death would be revealed to me.
So, you were *looking* for there to be an issue?
I was *asking* for truth.
And you believe a ghost revealed it.
I believe it was revealed to me.

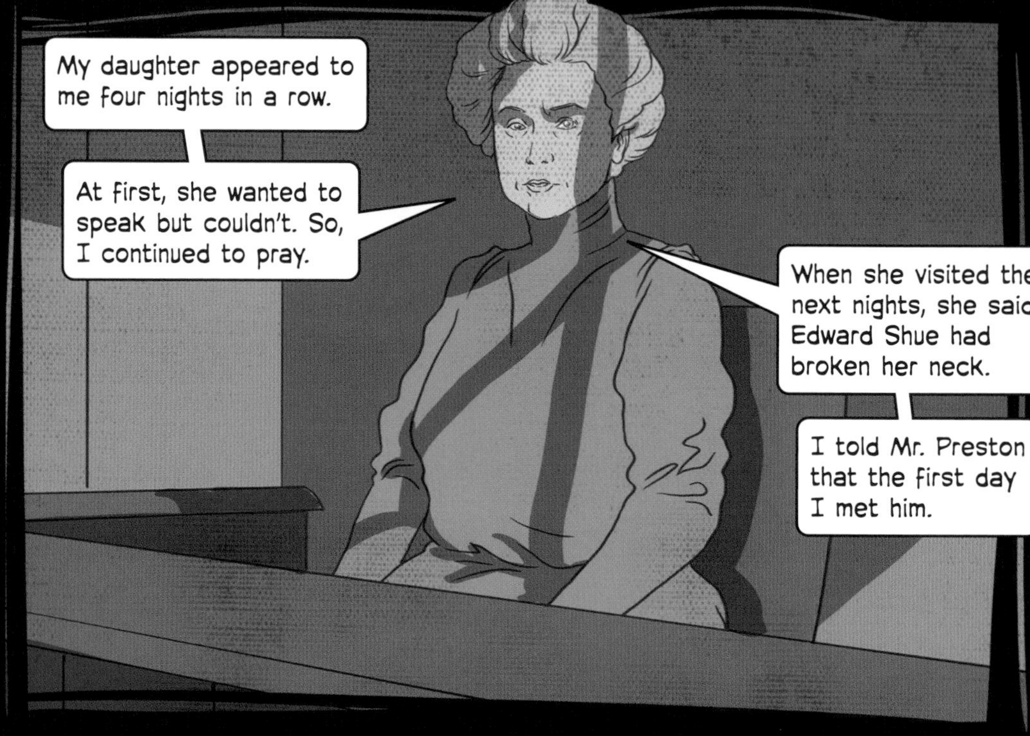
My daughter appeared to me four nights in a row.
At first, she wanted to speak but couldn't. So, I continued to pray.
When she visited the next nights, she said Edward Shue had broken her neck.
I told Mr. Preston that the first day I met him.

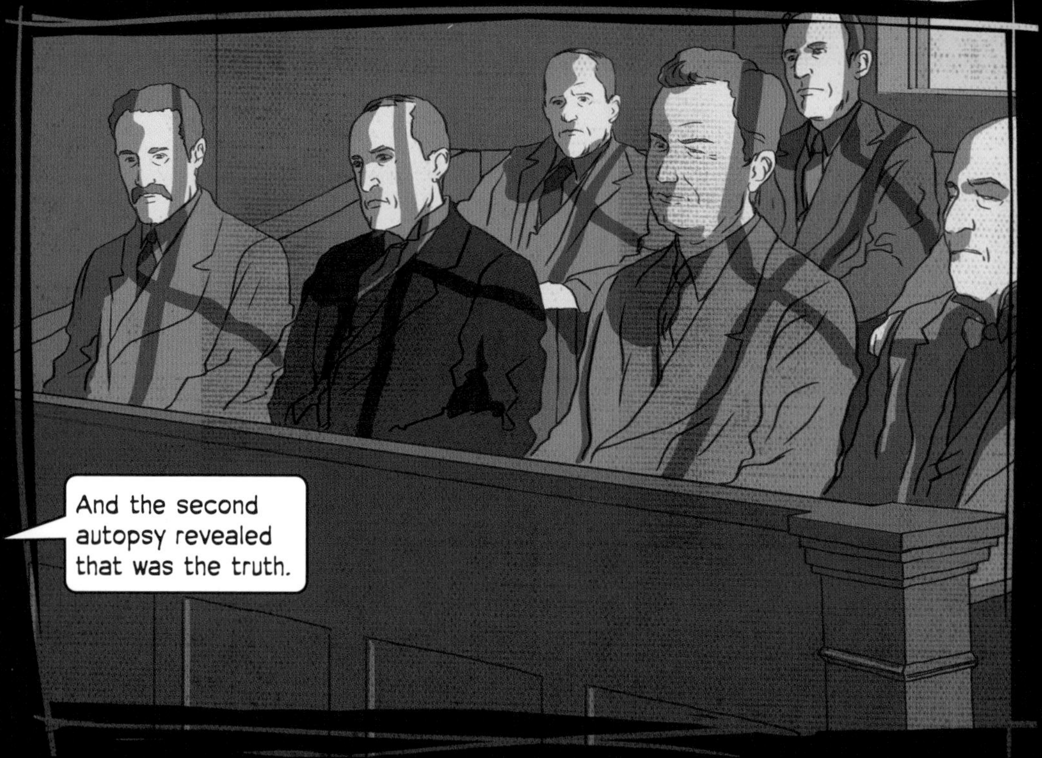
And the second autopsy revealed that was the truth.

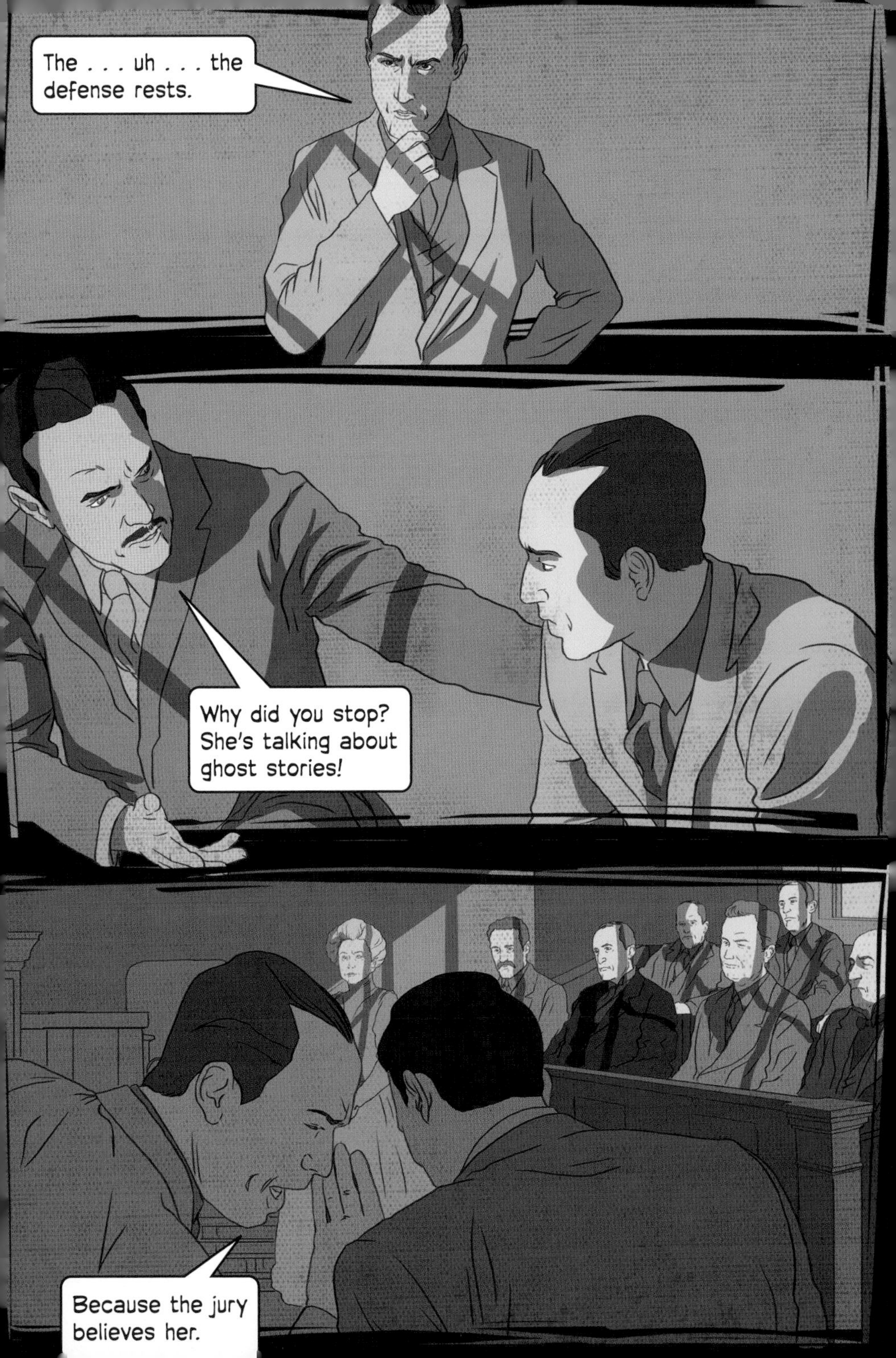
The . . . uh . . . the defense rests.
Why did you stop? She's talking about ghost stories!
Because the jury believes her.

# CHAPTER 5
# THE FINAL VERDICT

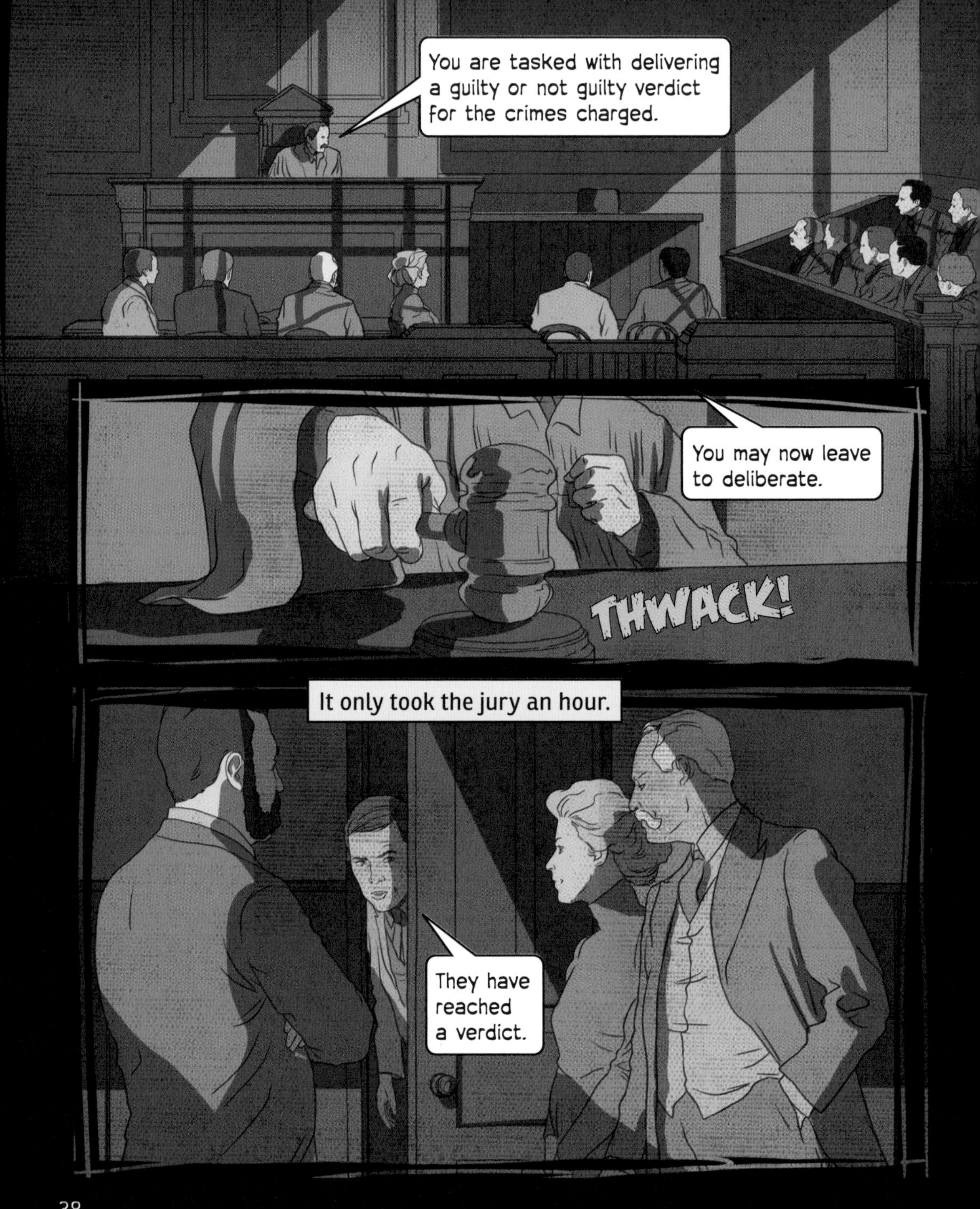
You are tasked with delivering a guilty or not guilty verdict for the crimes charged.
You may now leave to deliberate.
THWACK!
It only took the jury an hour.
They have reached a verdict.

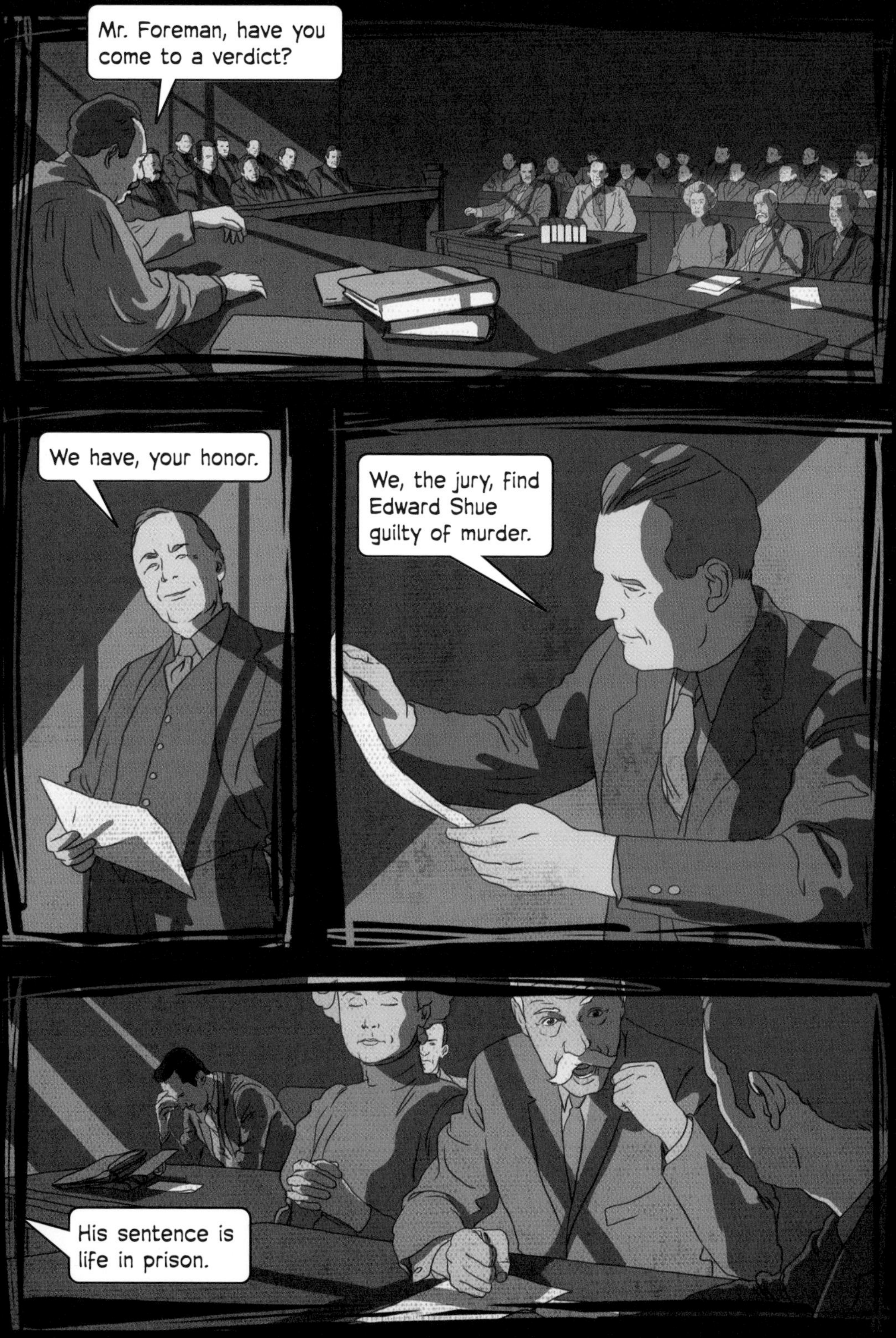
Mr. Foreman, have you come to a verdict?
We have, your honor.
We, the jury, find Edward Shue guilty of murder.
His sentence is life in prison.

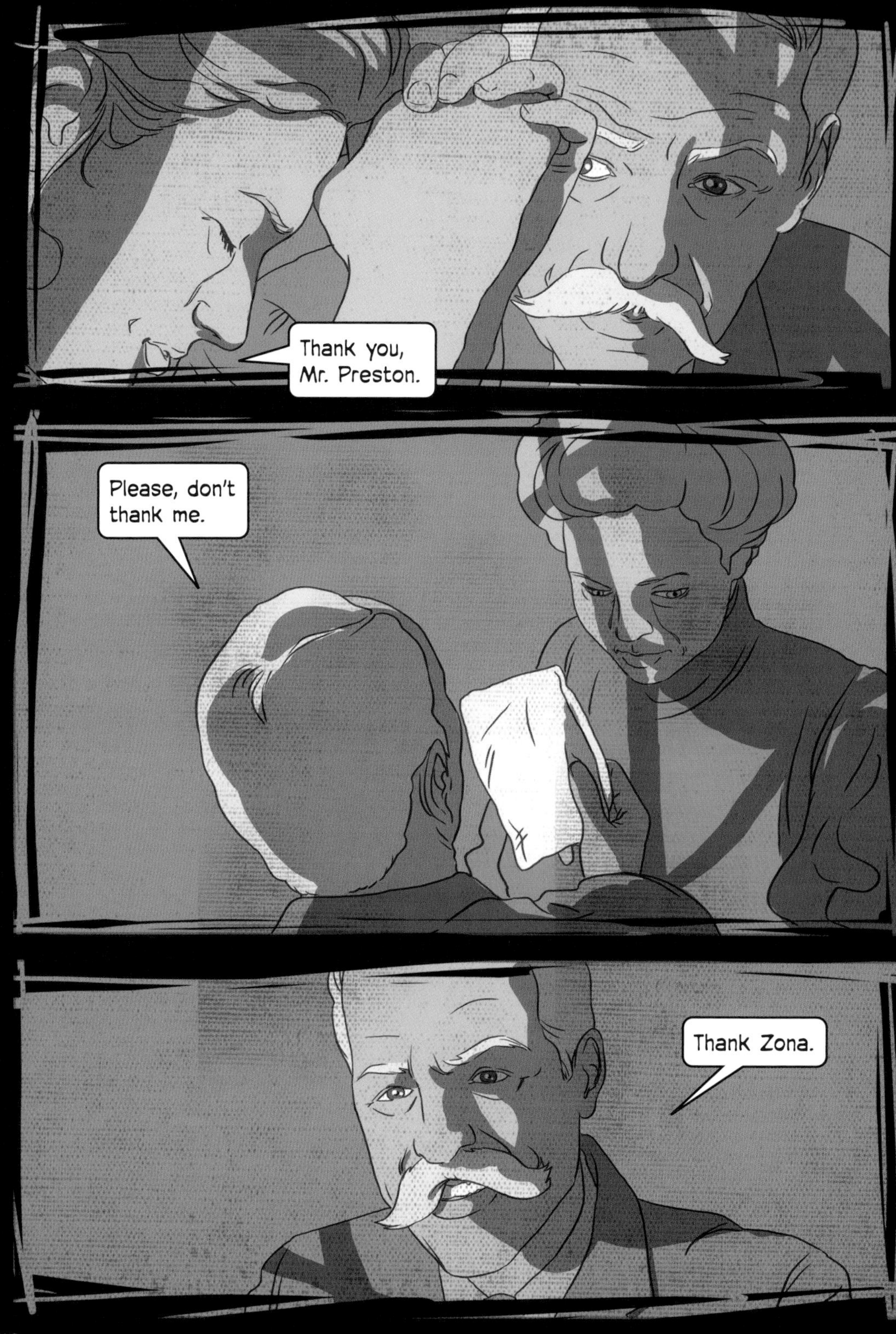
Thank you, Mr. Preston.
Please, don't thank me.
Thank Zona.

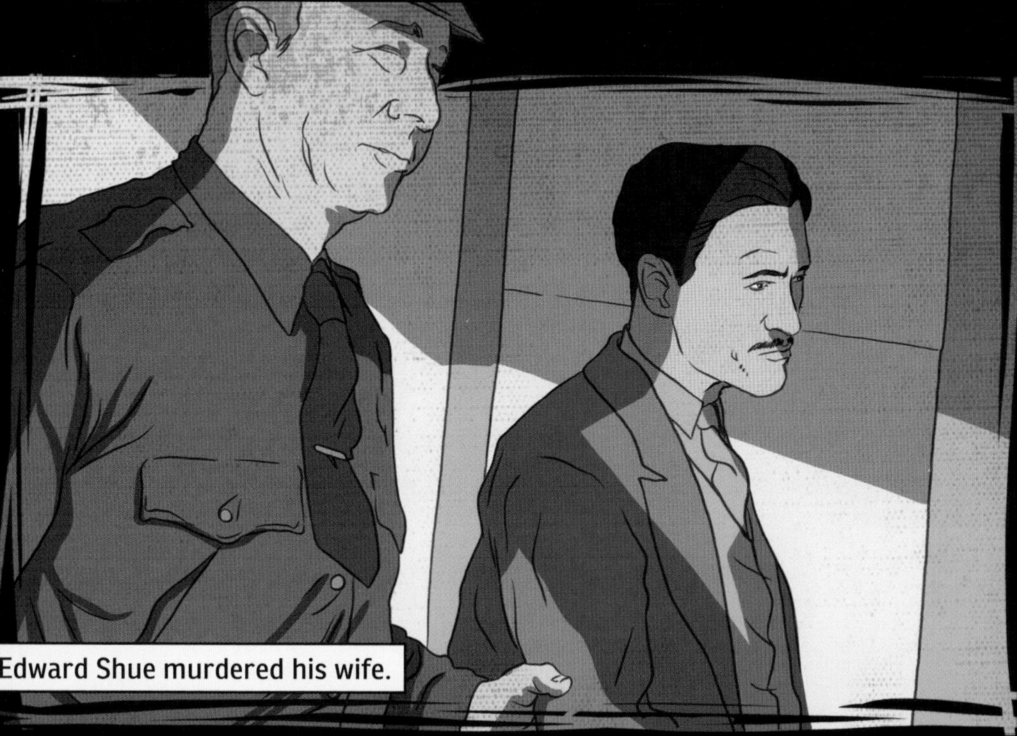
Edward Shue murdered his wife.

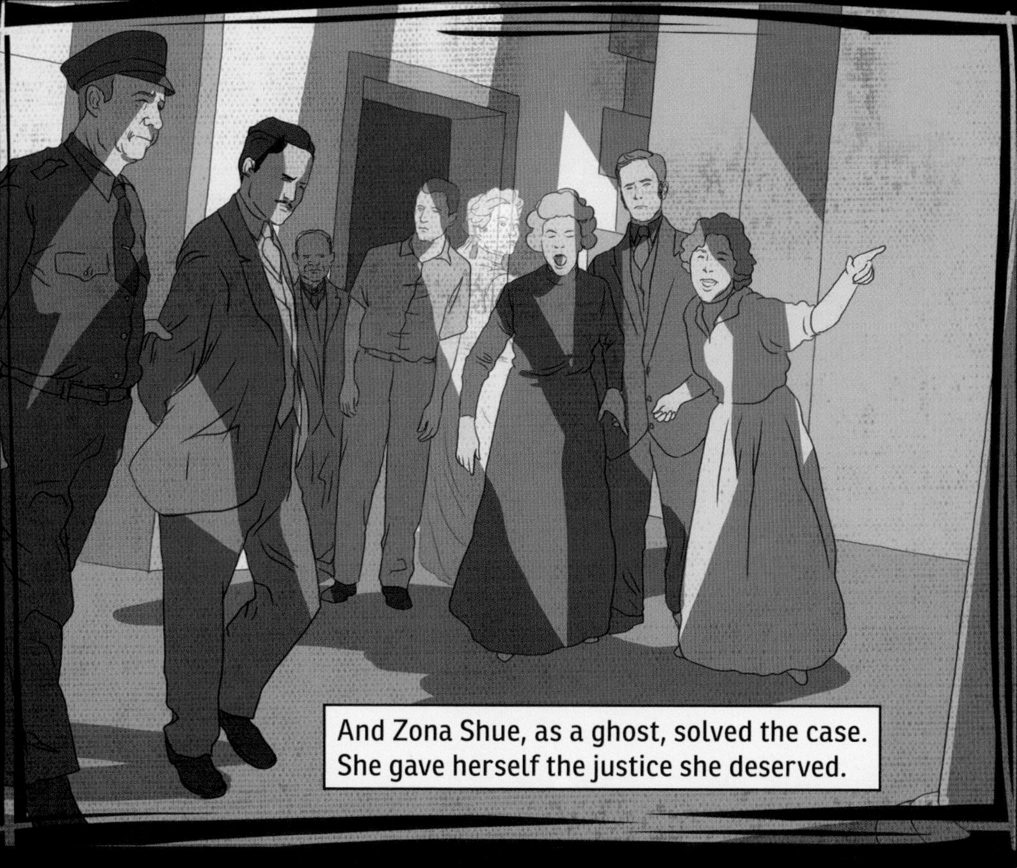
And Zona Shue, as a ghost, solved the case.
She gave herself the justice she deserved.

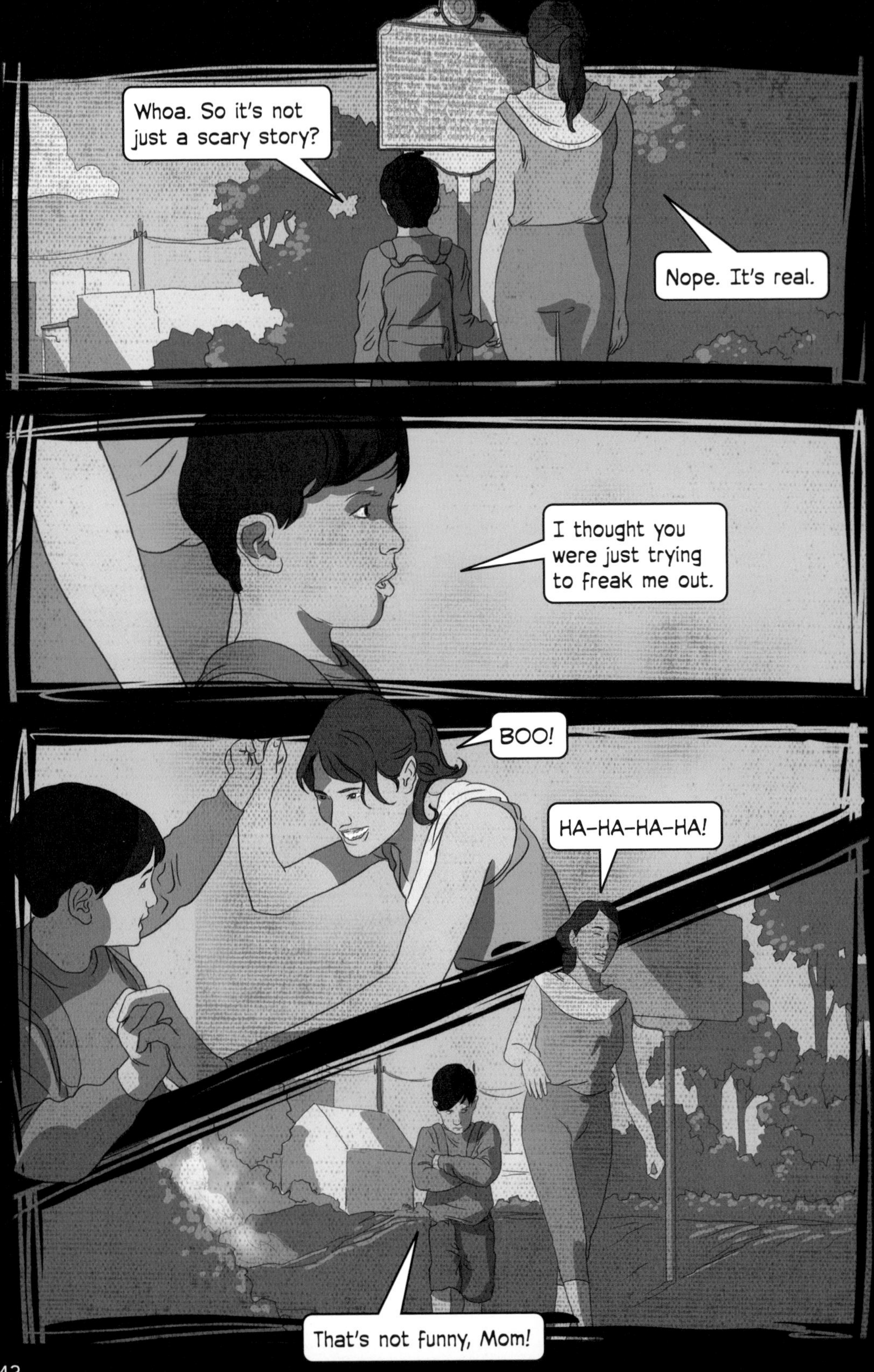
Whoa. So it's not just a scary story?
Nope. It's real.
I thought you were just trying to freak me out.
BOO!
HA-HA-HA-HA!
That's not funny, Mom!

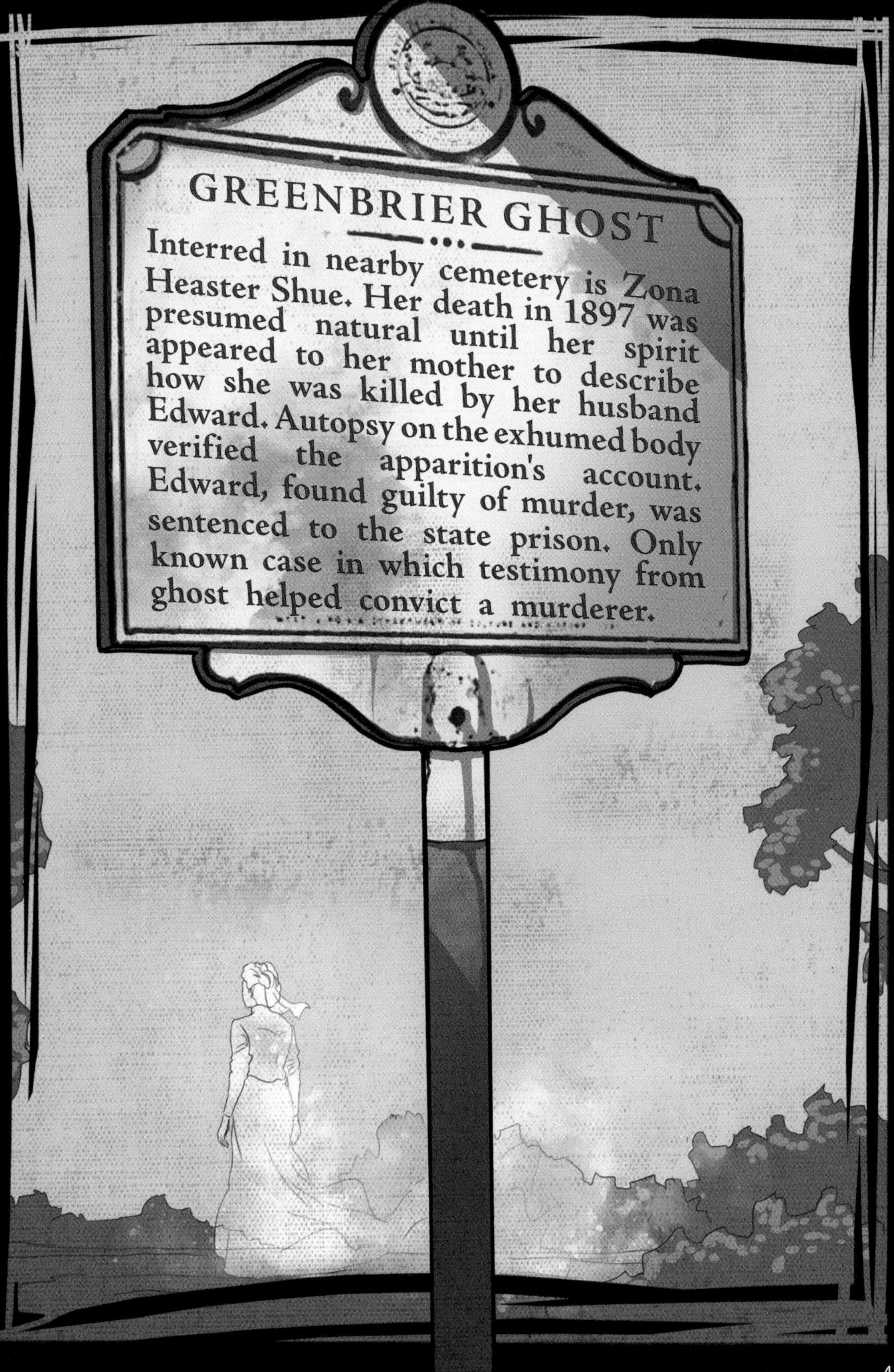
GREENBRIER GHOST
Interred in nearby cemetery is Zona Heaster Shue. Her death in 1897 was presumed natural until her spirit appeared to her mother to describe how she was killed by her husband Edward. Autopsy on the exhumed body verified the apparition's account. Edward, found guilty of murder, was sentenced to the state prison. Only known case in which testimony from ghost helped convict a murderer.

# MORE ABOUT THE GREENBRIER GHOST

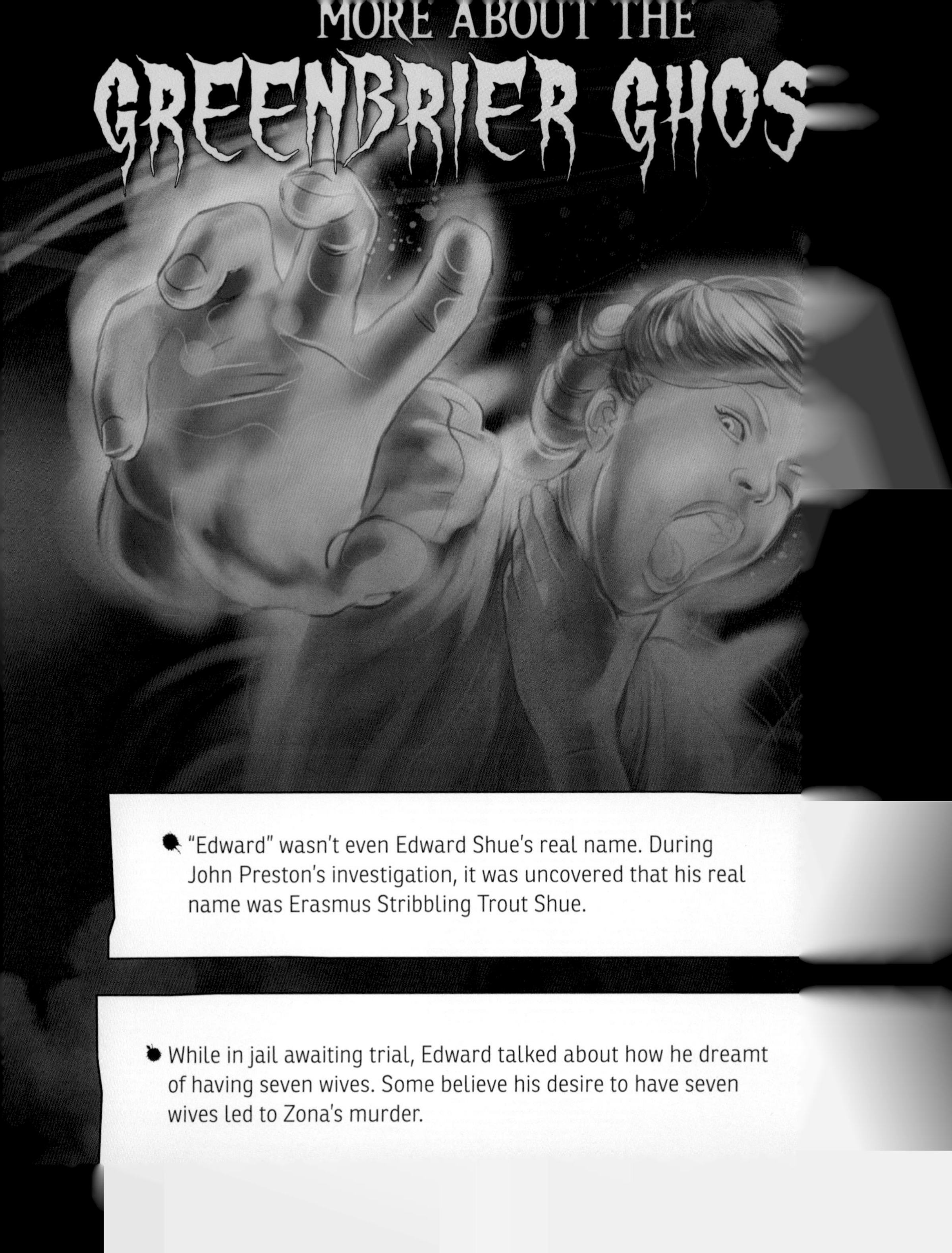

- "Edward" wasn't even Edward Shue's real name. During John Preston's investigation, it was uncovered that his real name was Erasmus Stribbling Trout Shue.

- While in jail awaiting trial, Edward talked about how he dreamt of having seven wives. Some believe his desire to have seven wives led to Zona's murder.

Preston brought up Mary Jane Heaster's visions of Zona because he wanted the defense attorney to question her. He was certain Mary Jane's firm belief in her story would win the jury over. His gamble paid off.

As Edward left the courtroom, a mob formed to harm him. The sheriff had to send the crowd away to safely take him to prison.

Edward only served about three years of his prison sentence before dying of what is believed to have been the flu.

The plaque seen at the end of the story is real! It stands at the Soule Chapel Methodist Cemetery in West Virginia.

# GLOSSARY

**autopsy** (AW-top-see)—a detailed study of a dead body to determine the cause and manner of death

**coroner** (KOR-uh-nur)—a medical officer who investigates deaths

**defense** (di-FENS)—a lawyer or team of lawyers that argues for the accused in a trial

**deliberate** (duh-LIB-uh-rate)—to consider something carefully

**examination** (ig-za-muh-NAY-shuhn)—a careful check of a person's medical condition

**jury** (JU-ree)—a group of people at a trial that decides if someone is guilty of a crime

**motive** (MOH-tiv)—a reason for doing something

**prosecutor** (PROS-ih-kyoo-tur)—a lawyer who represents the government in a criminal trial

**suspicious** (suh-SPISH-uhs)—expressing distrust

**verdict** (VUR-dikt)—a decision of a jury

**windpipe** (WIND-pipe)—a tube that connects the mouth and nose to the lungs; air goes in and out of the body through the windpipe

# READ MORE

Atwood, Megan. *The Greenbrier Ghost: A Ghost Convicts Her Killer.* North Mankato, MN: Capstone Press, 2020.

Fitzpatrick, Insha. *Chilling with Ghosts: A Totally Factual Field Guide to the Supernatural.* Philadelphia: Quirk Books, 2023.

Hoena, Blake. *The Voyage of the Flying Dutchman: A Ghostly Graphic.* North Mankato, MN: Capstone Press, 2024.

# INTERNET SITES

*Appalachian History.net: The Greenbrier Ghost*
appalachianhistory.net/2018/01/greenbrier-ghost.html

*Greenbrier Valley, West Virginia: The Greenbrier Ghost*
greenbrierwv.com/editorials/the-greenbrier-ghost

*West Virgina Explorer: The Full Tale of West Virginia's Remarkable Greenbrier Ghost*
wvexplorer.com/2022/07/25/greenbrier-ghost-zona-heaster-shue-west-virginia-wv

# ABOUT THE AUTHOR

Photo by Jarred Luján

**Jarred Luján** is a Mexican-American comic writer from the borderlands of Texas. He's a 2019 Mad Cave Studios Talent Search winner and a member of the inaugural 2022 DC Milestone Initiative class. Aside from writing, Jarred spends his time trying to convince his cats to be nice to him (his dog remains as loyal as ever).

# ABOUT THE ILLUSTRATOR

Photo by Francesca Labriola Pitch

**Alessandro Valdrighi** was born by the sea in beautiful Castiglione della Pescaia, Italy. He studied at the prestigious Accademia di Belle Arti (Academy of Fine Arts) in Florence and graduated with a bachelor's degree as a set designer. Alessandro learned to draw at an early age by copying comics and illustrations from books. He believes this is the reason he is now successful using multiple art styles. Alessandro has worked as a cartoonist, illustrator, and concept artist in both traditional and digital media. In 2011, he won a prize for his work on *Lágrimas en la lluvia*, which was honored as the best comic book publication in Spain. Alessandro lives and works in Siena, Italy, with his wife, two daughters, and a crazy cat.